D1001130

10/09 direct 32.95

THE RESTLESS EARTH

ROCKS
AND MINERALS

THE RESTLESS EARTH

THE RESTLESS EARTH

ROCKS AND MINERALS

Selby Cull

THE FRANKLIN INSTITUTE

CHELSEA HOUSE
PUBLISHERS
An imprint of Infobase Publishing

ROCKS AND MINERALS

Chelsea House
An imprint of Infobase Publishing
132 West 31st Street
New York NY 10001

Library of Congress Cataloging-in-Publication Data
Cull, Selby.
Rocks and minerals / Selby Cull.
p. cm.—(Restless earth)
Includes bibliographical references and index.
ISBN 978-0-7910-9702-1 (hardcover)
1. Rocks. 2. Minerals. I. Title.
QE431.2.C85 2008
552—dc22   2008027179

Text design by Erika K. Arroyo
Cover design by Ben Peterson

Printed in the United States of America

Bang FOF 10 9 8 7 6 5 4 3 2 1

This book is printed on acid-free paper.

Contents

▲ ▲ ▲

Looking
Into a Rock

▲ ▲ ▲

You are sitting on a rock right now. It is a big rock, so big that you, your classroom, your school, your town, and everything else—zebras, apple trees, polar bears, sneakers—can sit on top of it. We call it the Earth, but it is really just a big rock surrounded by empty space.

This **rock** is important. On it sits every plot of land that will grow your food, every drop of oil that will power your cars, every person you will ever know. On this one rock, you will spend every moment of your life.

But how much do you know about this rock? Where did Earth come from, and how did it form? Has it always been just like this?

If you wanted to know how this rock, our home, came to be, what would you do? Where would you look for clues?

To begin, you might look down. Every small rock you see is a reflection of what Earth has gone through. Glassy black rocks mark moments when the Earth's liquid insides spilled out onto its surface. Gritty, sandy rocks are the dead skin of the Earth, shed after years of wind and rain. Twisted, sparkly rocks formed deep in the bellies of mountains.

Every rock tells a story about the Earth. Some are violent stories: clashing **continents**, volcanoes, earthquakes. Some of them are quiet and slow: rain, wind, and time chipping away. All of them are hidden. But if you know how to read a rock's story, you can find the whole history of the Earth, laid out just under your feet.

MINERALS: THE STUFF ROCKS ARE MADE OF

So how do geologists read a rock's story? They start by looking closely at the rock. Rocks are made of small chips of stuff called **minerals**, such as quartz, mica, and talc. A rock can be all one kind of mineral or have dozens of kinds of minerals. Minerals are the building blocks of rocks.

To understand a rock, geologists must understand its minerals. Like everything else in the universe, minerals are made of **atoms**. There are 111 different types of atoms, called **elements**. Most of Earth's minerals are made of the elements silicon and oxygen.

But minerals are not just a bunch of atoms. If you tried to stack marbles to make them look like a castle, they would slide down and scatter all over your floor. Something has to make them stick together. Atoms also do not just stack—they stick together by forming **bonds**. When two or more atoms hook together with bonds, they form a **molecule**.

Molecules make up almost everything on Earth. Water is a molecule made when two hydrogen atoms bond with an oxygen atom. Chemists write this as H_2O: two hydrogen atoms (H_2) and one oxygen atom (O). Once formed, molecules behave differently, depending on their temperature. If the water molecules are hot enough, they bounce off each other, forming a gas such as air. If the water molecules are just warm or cool, they flow past each other without sticking, forming liquid water. If the water molecules are cold, they bind together and form solid water: ice. All solid objects—minerals, dogs, this book—are made of molecules bound together.

Rocks are often made up of many different minerals, like this diorite rock.

But this book is not a mineral, and neither is a dog. Minerals are special for five reasons:

1. **Minerals are solid.** Liquid water is not a mineral, but ice is. (Yes, ice is a mineral! Earth is too warm to allow the mineral ice to make up rocks, but beyond Earth, in the coldest parts of the solar system, ice is an important mineral. Whole planets are made of the mineral ice.)

2. **Minerals are only made by nature.** So this book cannot be a mineral.

3. **Minerals are not alive.** That rules out dogs. Minerals can "grow" as more molecules are added to their edges, but they do not grow like living things.

4. Each mineral is made of only *one* kind of molecule.
That is why a rock is not a mineral—it is made of too many different kinds of molecules.

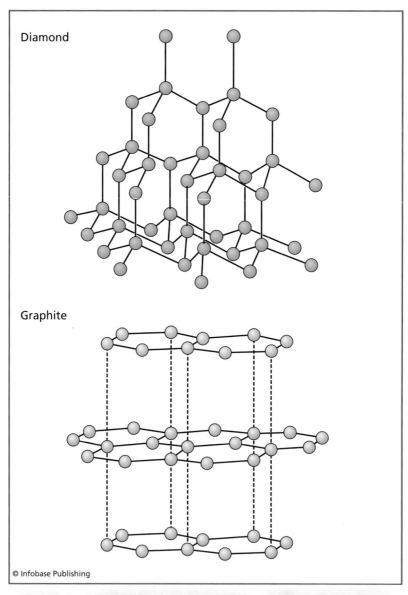

Diamond

Graphite

© Infobase Publishing

The above diagram shows the structures of two carbon minerals: diamond and graphite. Though they are both made of carbon atoms, diamond and graphite have very different properties.

5. Minerals have structure. The molecules are not just tossed together—they are stacked neatly, and bonds hold them together.

Structure is the most important part of a mineral. The type of molecule (H_2O, SiO_2, Al_2O_3, etc.) and the way the molecule is stacked determines what kind of mineral forms. For example, diamond is a mineral made of carbon atoms that form molecules like pyramids. The molecules stack together in a hexagon: a honeycomb-shaped circle that has six sides. Diamonds are the hardest natural objects on Earth—nothing can break or scratch them but another diamond. They are also some of the most expensive and beautiful minerals. But all of a diamond's beauty, worth, and usefulness depends on that honeycomb shape—on how its molecules are stacked.

Take another mineral: graphite. Graphite is the dark gray mineral in pencil "lead"—it is soft, dull, and about as undiamond-like as a mineral can be. But graphite is made of carbon atoms, just like a diamond. The reason pencils are not full of diamonds is that the carbon atoms of graphite are stacked differently. Instead of being in a diamond's pyramid structure, graphite's atoms are stacked in sheets, making graphite soft and easy to break. If the graphite were removed from a pencil and its molecules were restacked in that perfect honeycomb shape, the result would be a diamond.

RESTACKING MOLECULES: HOW A MINERAL GROWS

Of course, no one can just pull the atoms out of pencil lead and restack them. Diamonds only form in certain places. The place determines how the molecules will be stacked and what kind of mineral forms.

Graphite and diamond both grow underground, but diamonds form much deeper than graphite.

(continues on page 14)

The Case of the Shattered Crystal

One day in 1779, a man named René-Just Haüy stood in the beautiful study of his friend's French home and smashed a crystal on the floor. Haüy (who pronounced his name "ah-WE") had not meant to drop it. He had come to admire his friend's rocks and minerals, and one smooth crystal of calcite had accidentally slid from his hand.

René-Just Haüy looked down at the shattered crystal. Each piece was the same shape. This was weird. After all, if he had dropped a glass doll, it would not shatter into a hundred identical cubes. It would just have shattered. But somehow this crystal had broken into perfect bits.

René-Just Haüy was a scientist. He had spent years studying flowers and plants. Flowers and plants grow according to natural laws, which Haüy could understand by examining their shape. Haüy knew that, in nature, shapes happen for a reason. Now, looking down at his friend's shattered crystal, he wondered what laws could make crystals break into such perfect pieces.

Haüy spent the next several years smashing crystals. Some broke into perfect cubes, or cubes that leaned to one side. Some chipped into shapes like soccer balls, others into pyramids. Some snapped into shoebox-shaped crystals and pencil-shaped crystals. There were crystals that broke into thin plates, and crystals that broke into curving planes.

All this crystal smashing forever changed the way scientists look at minerals. Haüy had realized that when minerals break along a smooth plane, called **cleavage**, they reveal their internal structure. Suddenly, scientists could look *inside* minerals.

Every mineral is made of one kind of molecule stacked in a specific way. Haüy announced to the world that the way the molecules are stacked determines how the mineral will break. Sometimes he could distinguish one mineral from another based only on their cleavage. For example, in the mineral mica, the molecules form flat sheets. Each sheet is stacked on top of other sheets. When mica breaks, the sheets come apart, and the broken parts look like tiny plates.

By breaking crystals, Haüy could peer inside them, see how they had grown, and understand how one mineral differed from another. Today, René-Just Haüy is known as the father of **crystallography** (the study of crystals), because he accidentally smashed his friend's crystals—and because he knew what he was looking for.

Different rocks and minerals break in different ways. The property that describes how a rock breaks is called cleavage. a) Halite breaks into cubic shapes. b) Fluorite breaks into octahedral, or 8-sided, shapes. c) Mica flakes off in layers when it breaks.

(continued from page 11)

Being underground is not easy. Say a geologist dug a hole 6 feet (1.8 meters, or m) deep, put a pile of apples in it, and then piled the soil back on top. More than 6 pounds (2.7 kilograms, or kg) of soil would push down on every square inch of the apples and the overlying dirt might bruise the apples. If the geologist buried them in a hole that was 2,000 feet (610 m) deep, then more than 2,000 pounds (907 kg) of soil would push down on every square inch of apple. The apples would be squashed. The deeper the apples, the more squashed they become—but they are still apples.

The same thing happens to anything that is buried. As more soil and rocks are piled on top, the apples feel more **pressure**: the weight pushing down on them. If those apples—or any other plant or dead animal—were buried under miles of soil and rock, then something much more dramatic would happen: The molecules that make up the apple would break. The molecules would rearrange themselves and no longer make up an apple. When an object's molecules rearrange because of high pressure or high temperature, it is called **metamorphism**.

Diamond and graphite are both **metamorphic** minerals. Graphite forms when plants or animals—mostly made of carbon atoms—are buried about a mile underground. The rock and soil on top push down on the dead plants and animals so hard that the carbon atoms rearrange themselves into flat sheets. Diamonds form at much greater depths: under at least 100 miles (161 kilometers, or km) of rock. There, the pressure is so extreme that the carbon atoms arrange themselves into that special honeycomb structure. The honeycomb structure is so strong that a 1-inch-long (2.5 centimeters, or cm) diamond could support 40 full-grown elephants on top without breaking!

Many minerals form through metamorphism. The mineral garnet forms more than 10 miles (16 km) underground. They sometimes start as other minerals and change when they are buried. If the mineral quartz is buried under 4 miles (6.4 km) of rock, it turns into the mineral coesite. Deeper than about 20 miles (about 35 km), it turns into the mineral stishovite. Burying minerals deep underground is a good way to rearrange their molecules.

MINERALS FROM FIRE

So some minerals grow from other minerals. But how do minerals form in the first place? Most of Earth's minerals form in **lava**: the boiling-hot liquid that erupts from volcanoes. These minerals are called **igneous**, a Latin word that means "from fire."

Deep underground, the temperature is sometimes so high that rocks melt. (This is discussed in Chapter 4.) Melted rock, which is called **magma** while it is still underground, is like any other liquid: The molecules are so hot that they cannot stick together and instead go sliding past each other. Minerals cannot form in such a hot liquid.

But the magma does not stay hot forever. It moves slowly toward the surface of the Earth. Sometimes it erupts from volcanoes as lava. When the molecules hit the air, they cool down quickly, stacking as fast as they can to form minerals. Because they cool so fast, the minerals are small and close together. When this happens, it is hard to tell one mineral from another. **Basalt** is a type of rock made from minerals that cooled quickly.

Sometimes, though, the magma gets trapped underground. There, it cools slowly. Its molecules take their time stacking together to form large, and often beautiful, **crystals**. (A crystal is a well-shaped mineral.) **Granite** is a type of rock made from large minerals that cooled slowly underground. Architects like to use granite to design buildings, because they are often filled with huge, beautiful minerals. (Basalt and granite will be discussed in Chapter 5.)

MINERALS FROM WATER

A lot happens underneath Earth's surface. A hundred miles (161 km) below, molecules are rearranging themselves into the perfect honeycomb shapes of diamonds. Twenty miles (32 km) below, rocks are melting into magma and cooling into granites. A mile below, the molecules from dead plants and animals are rearranging to form graphite. And just a few feet below, water is flowing through tiny holes in the rocks.

Underground water is not as dramatic as diamonds, cooling magma, or broken molecules—but it is important for rocks. All rocks are full of holes: some microscopic, some so big they make caves and caverns. The water that flows through these holes is called **groundwater**.

Water can change things. It can make bread soggy, and it can make metal rust. It can also change rocks—especially if the water is hot. Oftentimes, groundwater will flow past magma sitting underground, perhaps under a volcano. The nearby magma warms the water, giving it more energy. As the hot water flows through the rocks, it chips off molecules from the minerals it touches. But as the water cools, the molecules reattach to different rocks. When they do, they form new minerals, called **hydrothermal** minerals. (*Hydro* means "water" and *thermal* means "heat.")

Some of Earth's most colorful minerals form this way. The brilliant blue mineral azurite and the forest-green malachite both form when hot water flows through rocks and deposits copper and other atoms.

Minerals can also form in cool water, if the right molecules are there. Most molecules will float freely in water until they find another molecule with which they can bond. In an ocean or lake, if the molecule CO_3 encounters an atom of calcium, they will combine instantly to form a mineral called calcite. Calcite is too heavy to float in the water, so it gently falls to the bottom. This is called **precipitation**, and the minerals that form when precipitation builds up are called **sedimentary**.

These are the three major ways that minerals form. Metamorphic minerals form deep underground; igneous minerals form from lava or magma; and hydrothermal or sedimentary minerals precipitate from water. Minerals can form in many other ways, as well. In catastrophic explosions, certain minerals form that form no where else on Earth. Some animals manufacture minerals to use as shells. The human body makes its own minerals, too: Bones are made of the mineral apatite. But the vast majority of minerals are metamorphic, igneous, hydrothermal, or sedimentary.

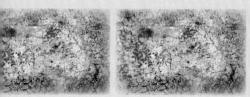

2

Identifying Minerals

▲ ▲ ▲

GEOLOGISTS SEEK TO UNDERSTAND THE EARTH: HOW IT FORMED, HOW it has changed, and what will happen to it in the future. They do this by examining rocks, and one of the most important clues they have is a rock's minerals. Some minerals only form in certain places. The mineral barite only forms from hot, underground water. When geologists find a rock that contains the mineral augite, they know that the rock came from a volcano. When they find the mineral sillimanite, they know that the rock formed through metamorphism.

This is fantastic news for geologists: By examining the minerals in a rock, they can tell how the rock formed. Of course, to do that, they need to know how to tell barite, augite, sillimanite, and all the other minerals apart.

So how do geologists identify a mineral? René-Just Haüy identified crystals by smashing them and measuring the shattered bits. For identifying most rocks, that is not a good approach. Instead, most geologists identify a mineral the same way they identify anything else: by how it looks. A geologist will pick up a mineral and, by looking at its color, shininess, and shape, will usually know which mineral it is. Sometimes, they will need to

18

perform a few tests to identify it, such as scratching, rubbing, weighing, and even licking it.

Try it. Find a mineral—preferably a large crystal, not embedded in a rock—and practice identifying it. Write down the mineral's properties (color, etc.) based on the discussion below, and then compare your description to mineral descriptions in Chapter 3.

COLOR

Color is usually the most obvious way to identify a mineral. Some are so vibrant that the colors are named for them: *ruby* red, *sapphire* blue, *emerald* green. But beware! Color is tricky. Rubies and sapphires may *look* different, but they are actually the exact same mineral: corundum.

Corundum is naturally colorless. But sometimes, as it grows, it accidentally traps a different molecule—chromium oxide—in between its normal molecules. When this happens, corundum turns red and is called a ruby. When the element titanium is trapped inside, corundum turns blue and is called a sapphire. The element iron can turn corundum yellow.

One mineral—four possible colors! Obviously, color alone cannot distinguish a mineral. We will have to look deeper.

LUSTER: HOW A MINERAL SHINES

Geologists call the way a mineral shines its **luster**. A **metallic** luster is the most obvious: It looks shiny and smooth, glinting like metal. Some minerals, like pyrite, are so metallic they almost look like mirrors.

A mineral can shine in lots of nonmetallic ways. Some of the most beautiful minerals have a **brilliant** luster. These minerals are usually made of molecules stacked tightly together, making them very strong. Jewelers cut brilliant minerals, like diamonds, to make them shine as much as possible. Some geologists describe a brilliant luster as **adamantine**, meaning "like a diamond."

Most minerals do not look like a diamond or like metal. Geologists describe minerals' luster using various words to

A mineral may also be defined by its luster, or how it shines.
(a) Pyrite displays metallic luster.
(b) Topaz crystals display adamantine luster.
(c) Smithsonite displays pearly luster.
(d) Quartz displays glassy luster.
(e) Chalcedony displays waxy luster.
(f) Pyroxene displays dull luster.

describe how they shine. Does the mineral look like glass? Does it look gritty like sand or silvery like a pearl? Does it look waxy or greasy or dull? There is no right way to describe how a mineral shines. Geologists look for the most descriptive word they can find. Find a good word to describe how shiny your mineral looks, and write that down under "luster."

Unfortunately, shininess and color do not provide enough information to identify a mineral. One type of mineral might shine in different ways, depending on how it formed. For example, the mineral pyroxene, an important mineral in rocks that form on the bottom of the ocean, can have a glassy, silky, or metallic luster. Since thousands of minerals can be glassy, silky, or metallic, luster is not enough to identify a mineral. We need to look still deeper.

HABIT: A MINERAL'S SHAPE

The next most obvious aspect of a mineral is its shape. Geologists call a mineral's shape its **habit**.

For some minerals, habit is a giveaway. For example, the mineral mica almost always forms in flat sheets. The sheets are stacked on top of each other like a pile of plates. This is called a **platy** habit, and it is characteristic of mica.

Yet, most minerals can have more than one habit, again depending on how and where the mineral grows. For example, the mineral hematite can look like a pile of blocks (**blocky** habit), a shoebox (**tabular** habit), or a bunch of grapes (**botryoidal** habit). Geologists combine their knowledge of a mineral's color, luster, and habit to make a guess at what kind of mineral it is.

Write down the shape of your mineral. Use whatever words best describe it. Here are some words that geologists commonly use:

An **acicular** crystal looks long, thin, and needle-like. Minerals like actinolite often have an acicular habit.

Aggregate minerals form as a bunch of tiny crystals, all clumped together.

Mineral Habits

Radial, such as wavellite

Bladed, such as kyanite

Acicular, such as mesolite

Botryoidal, such as hematite

Fibrous, such as sillimanite

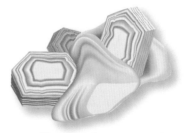

Platy, such as muscovite

Different minerals take different kinds of habits, or shapes.

An **amorphous** crystal has no structure at all. It looks like it melted into a puddle and solidified.

A **bladed** crystal looks like a sword blade: long, flat, and pointed at one end.

A **cubic** crystal looks like a cube, a **columnar** crystal looks like a column, a **fan** habit looks like a fan, and a **pyramidal** habit looks like a pyramid.

Fibrous crystals look like long strands of hair, all meshed together. Minerals like serpentine and sillimanite often have fibrous habits.

Minerals with a **radial** habit look like a star, with lots of little lines coming out of one point in the middle.

Sometimes color, luster, and habit are enough to identify the mineral. Sometimes they are not. If a geologist still does not know what the mineral is, then they start testing it.

TESTING: HARDNESS

The mineral talc is about as hard as a bar of soap. The mineral diamond is hard enough to cut steel. An easy way to tell talc and diamond apart is by their **hardness**.

Measuring hardness is difficult. In normal life, people say something is "kind of hard" or "not very hard." But geologists like to be precise, so they assign numbers to how hard something is, using a set of rules called the **Mohs' hardness scale**. A mineral's Mohs number describes how easily a person can scratch the mineral.

To test a mineral, geologists use common tools, such as a penny, steel knife, piece of glass, piece of steel, and quartz crystal, to try and scratch the mineral to identify it.

You can test your mineral's hardness with these steps:

1. Find a smooth, flat surface on the mineral.
2. Try to scratch the surface with your thumbnail. If you can do it, your mineral has a hardness of 1 to 2. If not:
3. Try to scratch the surface with your penny. If you can do it, your mineral has a hardness of 3. If not:

4. Try to scratch the surface with your steel knife. If you can do it, your mineral has a hardness of 4 to 5. If not:

5. Use the mineral to try to scratch the quartz. If it scratches the quartz, your mineral has a hardness of 8 to 10. If not:

6. Use the mineral to try to scratch the steel. If it scratches the steel, your mineral has a hardness of 7. If not:

7. Use the mineral to try to scratch the glass. If it scratches the glass, your mineral has a hardness of 6 to 7.

MOHS NUMBER	EXAMPLE OF A MINERAL WITH THIS HARDNESS	HOW EASY IS IT TO SCRATCH THE MINERAL?
1	Talc	A fingernail makes a deep scratch
2	Gypsum	A fingernail makes a shallow scratch
3	Calcite	A penny will scratch it
4	Fluorite	A steel knife will make a deep scratch
5	Apatite	A steel knife will make a shallow scratch
6	Feldspar	It can scratch glass
7	Quartz	It can scratch glass and steel
8	Topaz	It can scratch quartz
9	Corundum	It can scratch topaz
10	Diamond	Nothing can scratch it!

Say a mineral scratches glass but not steel. The mineral has a hardness of 6. But hundreds of minerals have a hardness of 6, so a geologist must combine knowledge of the mineral's color, luster, habit, and hardness to identify it.

If a geologist *still* does not know what the mystery mineral is, it is time to try another test: streak.

TESTING: STREAK

Minerals change color: Corundum can be red, blue, yellow, or clear. Some minerals also change color when they are crushed.

Geologists test the crushed-up color of minerals by using a **streak test**.

To perform a streak test, geologists use a piece of white tile. When a mineral is scraped against the tile, tiny flecks of the mineral are left behind, forming a streak. The color of the streak shows what color the mineral is when it is crushed.

For most minerals, the streak is the same as the regular color. But some minerals are different. The mineral calcite can be red, green, or blue, but it always has a white streak. The mineral

The Case of the Unknown Gems

Abu Rayhan al-Biruni was a meticulous scientist. He designed delicate instruments, took precise measurements, and recorded his results carefully. Unlike René-Just Haüy, whose initial discovery was an accident, al-Biruni was an experimental scientist.

Al-Biruni lived almost a thousand years ago, in the empire of Ghazna, near what is now the country of Afghanistan. It was a fascinating time to live in Ghazna. The empire was a center of learning, with universities, libraries, and many great scientists and philosophers. The sultan of Ghazna frequently marched his army south into India to raid the rich cities there. And when he returned, he brought **gems**.

Gems are minerals that have been carefully cut and polished until they shine. Gems like rubies, emeralds, and diamonds have fascinated people for thousands of years because of their beauty and rarity. The sultan of Ghazna laced his palaces with the gems he brought back from India. But al-Biruni was interested in gems for another reason.

Al-Biruni knew that identifying minerals could be difficult. Their colors change, and they grow and are cut in strange shapes. But, he

(continues)

(continued)

reasoned, no matter what the color or the shape of a gem, it should always be made of the *same substance*. That is what a mineral is: the same substance, stacked over and over again. And one thing about a substance almost never changes: its **density**. If al-Biruni could find a way to measure the densities of the sultan's gems, he could figure out what kind of minerals they were.

The density of a gem is its **mass** (or weight) divided by its **volume** (the amount of space it takes up). Calculating a gem's mass was easy: Al-Biruni just set it on a scale. But to determine a gem's volume, al-Biruni designed one of his famously delicate instruments. It was a glass dish, shaped like an ice-cream cone, and filled to the brim with water. Al-Biruni would place a gem in the glass dish and catch the water that overflowed the top. The amount of water that overflowed was the volume of the gem, and, by dividing the mass of the gem by the volume, al-Biruni calculated the gem's density.

Other scientists, like the Greek scientist Archimedes, had used this method to calculate volume before. However, Abu Rayhan al-Biruni was the first to apply it systematically to minerals. Al-Biruni calculated the density of 18 different minerals and published them in his book *Kitab al-Jawahir*, or *The Book of Pearls*. Even though he lived almost a thousand years ago, al-Biruni was such a careful and precise scientist that his measurements were admirably accurate even by today's standards.

René-Just Haüy discovered the fundamental order of a crystal's structure as he watched it shatter on the ground. But not all discoveries in science are an accident. Abu Rayhan al-Biruni illustrates another style of science: exact experimentation. He set his goal, designed equipment, took careful measurements, and recorded his results. Both methods are needed to help us understand how minerals are formed and structured.

hematite looks like metal but has a cherry red streak. The mineral sphalerite has a brown streak that smells like rotten eggs!

TESTING: TASTE

A few minerals have funny tastes. The mineral halite, for example, is made into table salt—and so tastes just like salt. The mineral epsomite tastes bitter. The mineral melanterite tastes sweet. The mineral borax tastes **alkaline**, like soap.

However, to taste a mineral, do not actually lick it! Some minerals are poisonous (like the neon blue mineral chalcanthite), and licking them can be dangerous. To taste a mineral safely, lick your finger, touch the mineral, and then touch your finger to your tongue. This should be enough for you to tell if the mineral has a taste. Few minerals taste like anything other than dirt, but those few are easy to identify using this method.

TESTING: DENSITY

Here's an easy test: Pick up two minerals of the same size, one in each hand. Which feels heavier? The heavier one is denser; it is heavy for its size. Metallic minerals, like hematite or magnetite, usually feel very heavy, even if they look small.

TESTING: SPECIAL POWERS

Some minerals have special powers. The mineral magnetite is **magnetic** and will attract a magnet. The mineral uraninite and the beautiful dark green mineral metatorbernite are **radioactive**. The mineral amethyst (a purple variety of quartz) will lose its color if thrown into a fire.

The most dramatic special power a mineral can have is **fluorescence**. These minerals glow when placed beneath a special **ultraviolet** lightbulb. (Ultraviolet lightbulbs are what make socks glow in a laser tag arena.) Different fluorescent minerals glow different colors: The mineral benitoite fluoresces bright blue, sodalite appears purple, and willemite turns neon green.

Ultraviolet light hits a mixture of fluorescent rocks and minerals in a museum display. This is an example of an unusual property that can help identify a rock or mineral.

NAMING YOUR MINERAL

Armed with a mineral's color, luster, habit, hardness, streak, and any special properties, geologists then compare their descriptions to a book or Web site that lists minerals and their properties. If they find a match, the mineral may be identified.

The next chapter will discuss some of the most common minerals on Earth, so start by comparing the description of your mineral to the descriptions in the next chapter.

3

Minerals:
THE USUAL SUSPECTS

▲ ▲ ▲

THOUSANDS OF MINERALS MAKE UP THE EARTH, BUT ONLY A FEW OF them are common. This chapter provides descriptions of some of Earth's most common and important minerals to help you identify minerals you find. Some are individual minerals, like quartz. Others are groups of minerals that all look about the same and so can be called by the same name.

QUARTZ

Quartz is a mineral made of two types of atoms: silicon and oxygen. Geologists write this out as SiO_2, meaning it has two oxygen atoms for every one silicon atom.

Remember, a mineral is a molecule (such as SiO_2) that is stacked in a certain way. In quartz, the stacking looks like a pyramid. This pyramid is formed by oxygen atoms, with one atom at each point. The silicon atom, which is tiny compared to the oxygen atom, is stuffed inside. Geologists call this pyramid the **silica tetrahedron**. (The word *tetrahedron* means "four faces.")

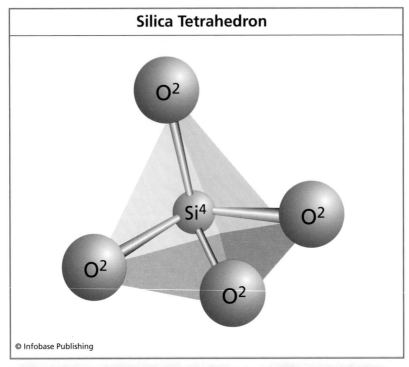

Silica Tetrahedron

© Infobase Publishing

Above is a diagram of silica tetrahedron, in which four oxygen atoms form a pyramid, with a silicon atom stuffed inside.

Identifying a Quartz Crystal

A quartz crystal will usually look like the Washington Monument—a tall pillar growing out of a rock. It is best identified by its crystal properties:

+ *Color:* Quartz is usually colorless and clear. While it grows, quartz can trap iron between its molecules. This makes the crystal turn purple, and we call it amethyst. If quartz traps molecules of manganese, the crystal turns pink, and we call it rose quartz. If it traps another form of iron, it turns yellow and is called citrine. If it traps aluminum, it turns gray, and we call it smoky quartz. Sometimes, as it grows, quartz traps water and is called milky quartz, since it looks like it has milk inside.

+ *Luster (Shininess):* Glassy, or slightly greasy.
+ *Habit (Shape):* Usually hexagonal (six-sided). When quartz grows like a pillar, it usually has a pointed top.
+ *Hardness:* 7—it can scratch glass and steel, but not another piece of quartz.
+ *Streak:* White.

Identifying Quartz in a Rock

The easiest way to identify quartz in a rock is by its color. The quartz will probably blend into the background, looking like a dull, plastic-like gray white blotch. It will look a little see-through, not a solid white or gray. Sometimes it shows the smooth, shell-like curve of its **conchoidal fracture**.

Quartz is found in most rocks, since it is one of Earth's most common minerals. It occurs in igneous rocks like granite and rhyolite, in sedimentary rocks like sandstone—which is almost entirely quartz—and in metamorphic rocks like gneiss. It does not occur in basalt or **gabbro**, and usually not in **andesite**, shale, limestone, slate, or marble either.

THE FELDSPAR GROUP

Feldspar is actually a group of minerals made of the same molecule, but stacked in slightly different ways. But, since they all look the same in a rock, we call them all feldspar. Geologists write out the feldspar molecule as $KAlSi_3O_8$—one potassium atom, one aluminum atom, three silicon atoms, and eight oxygen atoms.

Like quartz, the feldspar molecule is built on the silica tetrahedron. Four oxygen atoms sit on each corner of the pyramid, and a silicon atom is stuffed inside. In feldspar, though, only half of the pyramids are filled with silicon—the other half are filled with aluminum. Outside the tetrahedra, linking them together, are potassium atoms.

(continues on page 35)

The Case of the Electric Quartz

By smashing crystals, René-Just Haüy had figured out that minerals have internal patterns. But even after decades of smashing, studying, and scrutinizing crystals, Haüy could never understand what that pattern was. *How* do the molecules stack? Do they stack like oranges or like shoeboxes? In chains or in circles? Haüy died without ever knowing the answer.

A hundred years passed. Geologists found new minerals. They smashed them to see how they broke. They measured the angles made by their sides. They talked to chemists, who were just beginning to understand that atoms bond together to make molecules. But they could not figure out how molecules stack to form different minerals.

Then, in 1880, two young physicists came up with an unexpected solution. The physicists were Pierre and Jacques Curie: two brothers who did not care at all about minerals, but were fascinated by electricity. The brothers found that when they put a heavy weight on top of a quartz crystal, the quartz produced an electric field. The more weight they stacked on top, the more electricity the crystal produced.

The Curie brothers were physicists. They did not understand crystals, but they knew how electricity worked. Now, with this bizarre electric quartz, they used their understanding of physics to look inside the mineral and determine the shape of its molecule.

Electricity—the kind that powers your toaster—is like water. If someone pours a glass of water slowly into the sink, the water flows out in one constant stream. The stream is made of millions of tiny water molecules, all being pulled down by gravity. Electricity is a stream made of **electrons**: the tiny particles that usually circle the outside of an atom. Unlike water, though, gravity cannot pull on electrons. An electricity stream can "pour" up, down, or sideways. The only thing that can pull on an electron is an electric field.

Somehow, the Curie brothers' quartz crystal was making an electric field that could pull electricity through it. The Curies began experimenting. If they added more weight, the quartz made a stronger electric field. If they cut the crystal into different shapes, it made a different field. If they stretched the crystal, it made an electric field—in the opposite direction.

Slowly, the young brothers began to understand what was happening. They knew that not all atoms are created equal. Some have

(continues)

In the piezoelectric effect, a quartz crystal lattice is bent by pressure, causing the electrons in the atoms to huddle on one side of the molecule. This effect generates an electric field.

(continued)

extra electrons zipping around them, and others are missing electrons. The molecule that makes quartz is made of one silicon atom (which is *missing* four electrons) and two oxygen atoms (which each have an *extra* two electrons). When the Curies stacked their tiny weights on the crystal, they squished the quartz molecules, pushing the two oxygen atoms (and their extra electrons) to one side. Suddenly, all the extra electrons were huddled on one side of each molecule. Voilà! An electric field. The Curies named this phenomenon the **piezoelectric effect**: *piezo* is the Greek word meaning "squeezed."

Quartz is one of the few minerals that can produce "squeezed electricity." Its curious ability is due to its unique internal structure. The quartz molecule is a pyramid, with an oxygen atom at each of the four corners and a silicon atom nestled in the middle. This shape—the silica tetrahedron—is one of the most important in all geology. Most of Earth's major minerals consist of the silica tetrahedron, stacked in different ways. In quartz, the tetrahedra are stacked one on top of the other, so that each oxygen atom is the corner of two pyramids. In pyroxene, they form long chains of alternating pyramids: one points up, one points down, one up, one down. In **phyllosilicate minerals**, like biotite, they link together into long sheets that stack like paper. The versatile silica tetrahedron can stack and link in millions of different ways—giving rise to the fantastic diversity of Earth's minerals.

The Curie brothers went on to become legendary scientists. Jacques Curie became an accomplished physics professor at the University of Montpellier in France. Pierre Curie and his wife, Marie Curie, won the Nobel Prize in Physics in 1903 for their discovery of radioactivity. Today, few people remember that the brothers unraveled the mystery of the electric quartz, and fewer still realize how important that discovery was. By merging physics and geology, the Curies had discovered the nature of the most important pyramid on the face of the Earth.

(continued from page 31)

Identifying a Feldspar Crystal

Feldspar crystals are rarely beautiful. They tend to be dull, blocky crystals that look like shoeboxes. A few varieties of feldspar, though, are bizarrely colorful. When feldspar traps water and atoms of lead or copper in its crystal structure, it can turn a brilliant sea green. Geologists call this variety of feldspar amazonite.

+ *Color:* Earthy colors: white, pale pink, tan, yellow. The bright green amazonite is the exception, but it is rare.
+ *Luster (Shininess):* Dull to slightly glassy. Amazonite, however, looks shiny.
+ *Habit (Shape):* Remember, feldspar is actually several minerals, all with the same molecule, but stacked differently, so feldspar can have a variety of habits. The feldspar variety orthoclase usually has a blocky habit. The variety microcline

Pink feldspar, found in South Dakota

looks like long boxes that have been stepped on and are now slanting to one direction. The variety sanidine usually looks like a thick thumb.

+ *Hardness:* 6—it can scratch glass, but not steel.
+ *Streak:* White.

Identifying Feldspar in a Rock

Usually, if a rock has a pink mineral, it is feldspar. To be sure, though, look for the mineral's cleavage: how it breaks. When chipped, feldspar breaks at 90 degree angles that look like the corners of boxes. This is very different from quartz, which breaks in a smooth, clamlike curve.

Feldspar is found in most rocks—it is the most common mineral on Earth's surface, often found in igneous rocks like granite, where it forms large pink chunks.

Plagioclase in crystal form

THE PLAGIOCLASE GROUP

Plagioclase comprises two groups of minerals: albite, which is made of the molecule $NaAlSi_3O_8$, and anorthite, which is $CaAl_2Si_2O_8$.

Identifying a Plagioclase Crystal

Plagioclase crystals are rare. Plagioclase usually occurs in rocks, not as isolated crystals.

+ *Color:* Usually white. The rare variety called labradorite looks like a rainbow, with shifting pinks, yellows, blues, and greens.
+ *Luster (Shininess):* Glassy or pearly.
+ *Habit (Shape):* Bladed: When plagioclase does form crystals, they look like tiny blades.
+ *Hardness:* 6—it can scratch glass, but not steel.
+ *Streak:* White.

Identifying Plagioclase in a Rock

The easiest way to identify plagioclase in a rock is by its color: It looks like wisps of white that tend to be bright and solid, like

Quartz, feldspar, and plagioclase are all present in this rock.

chalk—unlike the glassy, colorless white of quartz. If the plagioclase **grains** are large enough, it will sometimes have tiny grooves in the surface, called **striations**. These are one indication of plagioclase.

Plagioclase is one of the most important minerals in basalt and gabbro, although it is often too tiny to be seen in these rocks.

THE PYROXENE GROUP

Pyroxene is a group of minerals, each made of a different molecule, but arranged in the same way: long chains. The chain structure is what makes a mineral belong to the "pyroxene group."

Identifying a Pyroxene Crystal

The pyroxene group includes many minerals, but because they all look the same, geologists call them all pyroxene.

+ *Color:* Usually dark: black, brown, dark gray. The variety jadeite is a pale green, ferrosilite can be green, and the rare but beautiful wollastonite is usually snow-white; however, in general, pyroxenes tend to be very dark.
+ *Luster (Shininess):* Glassy.
+ *Habit (Shape):* Most pyroxene crystals are blocky, but jadeite and wollastonite look like millions of tiny fibers, all bundled together.
+ *Hardness:* Different pyroxene minerals have different hardnesses, but it is usually around 6.
+ *Streak:* The pyroxene variety diopside is white-green, augite is green-gray, jadeite white, and enstatite gray. In short, streak is a not a good way to identify a pyroxene mineral—there are too many possibilities.

Identifying Pyroxene in a Rock

Pyroxene is found in many igneous rocks, where it is the only dark, square mineral. But it usually only occurs in dark-colored rocks—almost never in a light-colored rock like granite.

Pyroxene can sometimes look like other dark minerals, like amphibole or mica. The difference is that amphiboles usually look like needles, micas usually look like tiny stacked Frisbees, and pyroxenes usually look like thick, stubby thumbs.

THE MICA GROUP

Mica is another group of minerals. Each mineral is made of a different molecule, but they are all stacked the same way: in long, thin sheets. The sheets stack together like a stack of paper, making mica minerals easy to identify; they flake off in tiny sheets.

Identifying a Mica Crystal

Mica minerals can form large crystals inside rocks. They are easy to identify, because they look like sheets of paper and are so shiny, they are almost blinding.

+ *Color:* White, gold, green, pink, black. Usually, very dark mica is a variety called biotite, which is rich in iron and magnesium. Lighter micas are usually muscovites, which do not have iron and magnesium.
+ *Luster (Shininess):* Shiny! Micas are some of the shiniest minerals. When tilted just right, they shine like freshly polished metal.
+ *Habit (Shape):* Platy, or stacked in sheets. Micas are usually described as books. They form tiny books made of hundreds of stacked "pages," which can flake off when rubbed. Geologists call this shape tabular.
+ *Hardness:* 2 or 3—a penny will scratch them.
+ *Streak:* Colorless.

Identifying Mica in a Rock

Mica is easy to identify in a rock: It is the shiniest mineral there. The individual minerals are shaped like books, with pages that flake off easily.

Muscovite is rarely found in volcanic rocks like andesite or rhyolite, but biotite is common in granites.

THE AMPHIBOLE GROUP

Amphiboles are another group of minerals. Every amphibole mineral is made of a different molecule, but they all have the same structure: two long chains of molecules connected together like railroad tracks. Like most minerals, amphiboles are made of the silica tetrahedron, with atoms of magnesium, iron, calcium, or aluminum filling in the holes and gaps.

The most famous mineral in the amphibole group is hornblende.

Identifying an Amphibole Crystal

Amphibole crystals are rare. Amphibole is usually found in rocks.

+ *Color*: Usually dark. Hornblende is dark green to black. The metamorphic amphibole glaucophane is sky blue. The beautiful calcium-amphibole actinolite is a vibrant green, and the bizarre and rare riebeckite is midnight blue.
+ *Luster (Shininess)*: Silky or pearly.
+ *Habit (Shape)*: Usually acicular or fibrous When amphiboles form crystals, they tend to be long and needle-like, bundling together like quills on a porcupine. Sometimes they also form large, blocky chunks.
+ *Hardness*: 5 to 6—they can scratch glass, but not steel.
+ *Streak*: Hornblende has a colorless streak, glaucophane's streak is a gray blue, and riebeckite's streak is white.

Identifying Amphibole in a Rock

Amphibole is usually the only dark, needle-like mineral in an igneous rock. As compared to amphiboles in the same rock, pyroxenes look more like blocks, and micas look like flaky sheets.

Asbestos is a form of amphibole in crystal form.

Amphiboles rarely make up basalts or gabbros, but horn-blende is common in granites and andesites. Actinolite, tremo-lite, glaucophane, and riebeckite—all amphiboles—only occur in metamorphic rocks.

OLIVINE

Olivine is one of the most important minerals on Earth. It is the mineral that makes up Earth's mantle, which is discussed in Chapter 4.

Olivine is made of a molecule with silicon, oxygen, and either magnesium, iron, or a little of both. When the molecules stack, they look like a checkerboard: silica tetrahedron, magnesium, silica tetrahedron, magnesium, and so on.

Identifying an Olivine Crystal

Olivine crystals are rare—they are usually found only embedded in rocks.

+ *Color*: Olive green.
+ *Luster (Shininess)*: Glassy.
+ *Habit (Shape)*: Rounded balls or tiny grains that look like green sugar.
+ *Hardness*: 7—they can scratch glass and steel, but not quartz.
+ *Streak*: Colorless.

Identifying Olivine in a Rock

Olivine is usually easy to see in igneous rocks where it is olive green. It usually looks a little transparent like green-tinted glass. Olivine is common in basalt and gabbro, but is usually too small to see. It does not occur in granite. The rare and strange-looking rock **peridotite** is made almost entirely of olivine.

CALCITE

Calcite is one of the few common minerals that are not based on the silica tetrahedron. Instead, calcite is made of the elements calcium, carbon, and oxygen. It is the stuff of which seashells are made.

Identifying a Calcite Crystal

Calcite can form oddly misshapen crystals, but usually it is only found in rocks.

+ *Color*: Calcite can be many colors, but, in its pure form, it is colorless. Since it usually forms in water, it often incorporates other bits of matter that were floating near it. Extra copper will turn calcite green, iron will turn it pink or yellow, and carbon will turn it gray. Obviously, color is not the best way to identify it.
+ *Luster (Shininess)*: Glassy.
+ *Habit (Shape)*: Tabular or rhombohedron; a shape like a squished shoebox.
+ *Hardness*: 3—a penny will easily scratch it, but a fingernail will not.
+ *Streak*: White.

Calcite can come in many different colors, but its basic habit and the presence of a streak are the same in all forms of calcite.

Identifying Calcite in a Rock

Curiously, the best way to identify calcite in a rock is to dab some hydrochloric acid on it: It will fizz. The acid breaks down the bonds between the carbon and oxygen and recombines them as carbon dioxide gas, which bubbles away. Most professional geologists carry small bottles of acid with them to identify calcite.

Most people do not carry around acid, though, so the best way to identify calcite is by its habit. It will look like a shoebox that someone has stepped on: slightly squished to one side.

Calcite turns up in sedimentary rocks like limestone, but rarely in igneous or metamorphic rocks.

GYPSUM

Gypsum is another common mineral that is not based on the silica tetrahedron. Gypsum is made of a molecule with calcium, sulfur, oxygen, and water. It only forms in sedimentary rocks, usually as a result of the evaporation of water.

Gypsum crystals

Identifying a Gypsum Crystal

Gypsum crystals can be large and beautiful. They often grow in the desert, in sands where water pools and then evaporates, leaving behind the calcium, sulfur, and oxygen needed to make gypsum.

+ *Color*: Usually colorless or pink, but it can be yellow or brown also.
+ *Luster (Shininess)*: Glassy or pearly.
+ *Habit (Shape)*: Usually tabular and flat, like little scales on a stegosaurus.
+ *Hardness*: 2—a fingernail will scratch it.
+ *Streak*: White.

Identifying Gypsum in a Rock

Gypsum rarely occurs in rocks.

GARNET

Garnet is one of the most famous metamorphic minerals. It only grows in metamorphic rocks, as the heat and pressure become too great for other minerals to survive.

Identifying a Garnet Crystal

Garnets are well known as polished gemstones, but they are also easy to identify in their raw forms.

+ *Color*: There are many different types of garnet, each distinguishable by its color. Reddish black garnet is pyrope, brown is almandine, brownish red is spessartine, and grossular can be yellow or pink.
+ *Luster (Shininess)*: Glassy.
+ *Habit (Shape)*: Habit is the easiest way to identify garnets—they look like tiny soccer balls.
+ *Hardness*: 7—they can scratch glass and steel, but not quartz.
+ *Streak*: Colorless.

When a rock contains garnet *(top)*, it is easy to identify due to its dark red color *(bottom)*.

Identifying Garnet in a Rock

Garnets are easy to spot in a rock. They look like tiny brown or red soccer balls. They are only found in metamorphic rocks.

IRON OXIDES

Iron oxides are a group of minerals that include hematite, goethite, magnetite, and many others. They form when iron atoms combine with oxygen atoms, making strange metal crystals.

Identifying an Iron Oxide Crystal

Iron oxide crystals are usually distinctive. They look like strangely shaped chunks of metal.

+ *Color*: Most iron oxides are metal gray, but goethite can be a brown-yellow and hematite is often reddish brown.
+ *Luster (Shininess)*: Metallic.

Hematite

+ *Habit (Shape)*: Hematite usually forms crystals that look like bunches of grapes (botryoidal). Magnetite will look like two end-to-end pyramids. Goethite usually does not form crystals, but appears as a messy yellow-brown smear on rocks.
+ *Hardness*: 5 to 6—a steel knife can scratch them.
+ *Streak*: Hematite is identified by its cherry red streak. Goethite's streak is yellow-brown. Magnetite's streak is black.

Identifying Iron Oxides in a Rock

The easiest way to identify magnetite in a rock is to find a magnet. If the magnet is drawn to the rock, then the rock has magnetite in it. Hematite is characterized by its cherry red streak, and goethite by its yellow-brown color and crusty appearance.

Iron oxides usually form as rust on top of other minerals, but sometimes magnetite or hematite will form in igneous rocks.

CLAYS

Clays are the garbage of the mineral world. When rain, snow, wind, and time chip off bits of other minerals and wash them away with water, clays form. The world is covered with dozens of kinds of clays, but only a few are actually important. We use the clay mineral kaolinite to make pottery, and talc to make talcum powder.

Identifying a Clay Crystal

Clays usually do not form crystals.

+ *Color*: The clay kaolinite is white, and talc is apple green.
+ *Luster (Shininess)*: Dull, earthy.
+ *Habit (Shape)*: Clay minerals usually look like clay: tiny flakes and grains.
+ *Hardness*: 1 to 2—a fingernail will scratch them.
+ *Streak*: Usually white.

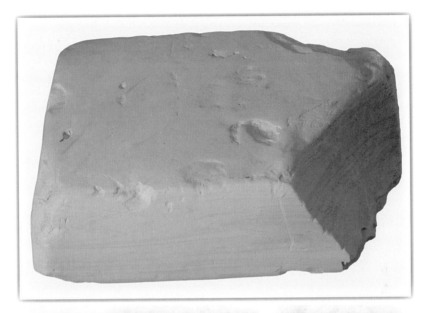

This kaolinite, a form of clay, was found in Bennington, Vermont.

Identifying Clays in a Rock

The easiest way to identify a clay is by its soft, muddy appearance. Talc will sometimes form long bundles that look like ponytails, but these are rare.

READING A MINERAL'S STORY

A geologist picks up a rock and discovers that it contains quartz, feldspar, and plagioclase. Now the fun begins—now the geologist can interpret them. Are the quartz crystals long, large crystals that had lots of space and time to grow? Or are the crystals tiny, stubby blocks that grew quickly? If the quartz is in an igneous rock, are the crystals tiny flecks of quartz that grew quickly, perhaps in cooling lava? Or are they huge knobs of quartz that grew slowly underground? If the quartz is in a sedimentary rock, are the quartz minerals smooth and rounded? If so, they probably rolled around in rivers and streams for a long time before form-

The Case of the Skinned Gazelle

Quartz was an important mineral for early humans. To show just how important, the famous archeologist Louis Leakey once used it to skin a gazelle.

It was 1953, and Leakey had discovered tools made of quartz and other minerals at a cave called Olduvai Gorge in eastern Africa. The quartz tools were carved almost 2 million years ago, and Leakey concluded that early humans, our ancient ancestors, had carved the quartz and used the tools to hunt and skin gazelle.

Other archeologists were skeptical. Early humans might have *thrown* rocks at animals to hunt them, but was quartz sharp enough to *skin* an animal? To show how sharp these quartz tools could be, Leakey arranged a competition. He and another archeologist would each skin a dead gazelle. Leakey would use one of the "primitive" quartz tools. The other archeologist would use a steel knife.

The quartz won.

Quartz is such an excellent tool because of the way it breaks. When early humans chipped two chunks of quartz together, small flakes of the mineral would break off, forming a curved surface, like the inside of a shell. That shell shape is called a conchoidal fracture, and its edge is as sharp as a knife. In the years before humans began to use metal, our ancestors relied on quartz and a few other minerals to kill prey and clean it up afterward.

Today, the distinctive conchoidal fracture is a handy clue to identify quartz. Just look for small chips in the surface, shaped like the smooth, curved insides of a clamshell.

ing a rock. Are the minerals strange colors? Did they incorporate iron, or carbon, or some other element as they grew?

By looking hard at the minerals and thinking about how they grew—quickly, slowly, in lava, in water, underground—geologists begin to understand a rock. Of course, geology's ultimate goal—understanding all the rocks on Earth—is not quite so easy.

4

Making Rocks

▲ ▲ ▲

Minerals are made of molecules. The molecules must be stacked just right. Otherwise, they slide apart like a pile of marbles. The perfection and beauty of a mineral lies in its elegant structure. Like a snowflake, each mineral is finely tuned to withstand the stresses of the outside world.

Rocks, by comparison, are a mess. They have no internal structure. A rock is literally a glob of minerals, glued together by **mud** or packed together by pressure, like snowflakes packed down to make a snowball. The beauty of a rock is not that it is precisely ordered like a mineral—what makes a rock unique is that it is constantly changing. All rocks, all across the Earth, are changing every day.

Of course, you could not observe how a rock changes by staring at it for a few minutes. A rock will be the same on Friday as it was on Monday. But if a geologist could sit and watch for a million years, or 100 million years, he or she would see the rock, and the entire world, change around him or her.

To understand why rocks change, geologists need to understand how the Earth works: how rocks are born from the deepest belly of the Earth; how they migrate, are crushed and cooked, are molded into mountains, and bashed and broken into beaches; and how they are eventually, at the end of their days, consumed again into the very center of this planet.

That is where a rock's story starts and ends: the center of the Earth. So that is where we must go ourselves. Though no human has been able to physically reach the center of the Earth—we do not currently have the right tools to reach beyond a few miles under the surface—it is easy to dig that deep using our minds. We might take a while to get there, though—it is a very long way down.

TO THE VERY CENTER OF THE EARTH

Look down. Under your feet is a floor, and under that floor is rock, and lots of it. If you pulled out a shovel right now and started digging, you would dig through more than 8,000 miles (12,875 km) of rock before popping out at the other side.

We do not need to go that far. To reach the center of the Earth, called the **core**, we only need to dig down about 4,000 miles (6,437 km). So grab a shovel and let's go.

When you start to dig, the first thing you will find is dirt. The outside of the Earth is covered in dirt that geologists call **sediments**: tiny bits of rock that were broken off mountains by wind and rain. Sediments can be dirt, sand, or dust, but they were all once rock. As we continue our story, we will see that they will all become rocks again someday, though this will not happen any time soon.

Keep digging. In some parts of North America, you will have to dig through many feet of dirt. In other parts, you might find just an inch or two. Eventually you will run out of dirt and will hit rock. Your shovel is of no use anymore. Now it is time to pull out a jackhammer to dig deeper.

North America is made of hundreds of different kinds of rock, but most of these lie just on the surface. If you keep jackhammering straight down, eventually you will find the rock that makes up almost all of North America: a pale pink rock called granite. This is the rock that underlies all of Earth's continents: Africa, Antarctica, Asia, Australia, Europe, and North and South America.

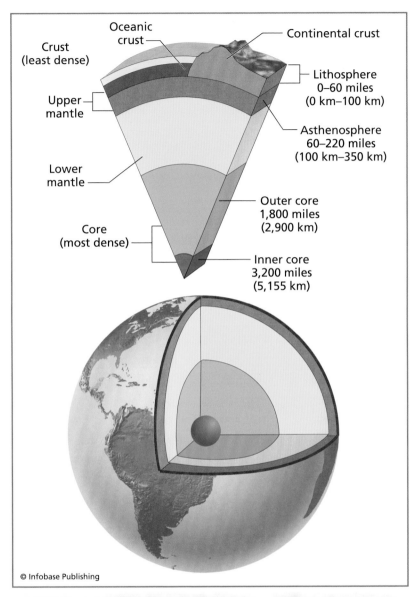

The above diagram shows the layers in the Earth.

Put down your jackhammer for a moment and take a look around this giant hole you have dug. Granite is made of the minerals quartz, feldspar, mica, and sometimes a few others. They will not be the perfect crystals that René-Just Haüy examined. The minerals in your hole will look like blobs the size of your thumb. But all that quartz and mica is what makes the rock sparkle. Architects love to design banks and giant, shiny office buildings out of granite because it is one of the most beautiful rocks of all. The next time you are in a bank, look at the walls. If they are a pale pink stone with large pieces of quartz, you will know where they came from. This sparkly, pale pink stone is the rock that supports our entire continent.

But we are still nowhere near the core, so turn that jackhammer back on. We have almost 20 miles (32 km) of granite to dig through. This is known as Earth's **crust**: the outer layer of the Earth, which is like the shell around a hard-boiled egg. The Earth has two kinds of crust: **continental crust**, which underlies the continents, and **oceanic crust**, which underlies the oceans. Oceanic crust is made of the rock basalt and is much thinner than continental crust—just about 4 miles (6.4 km) thick, instead of 20 miles (32 km). We will spend time in the oceans later. For now, keep on digging.

We are getting deeper now. As you jackhammer straight down, you will start to feel warm. The center of the Earth is fiery hot, and the closer we get, the warmer you will become. The rocks down here are also under a lot of pressure: The weight from all those rocks on top of them is pushing them down, squeezing and breaking them. The granite is full of cracks, called **faults**, where the extreme pressure has broken the rock.

When you break through the bottom of the crust, you will find the next layer of the Earth: the thickest layer, called the **mantle**. It is almost 2,000 miles (3,219 km) thick. You will know when you have reached the mantle, because your jackhammer will break open the rocks—and the rocks will ooze right back together again.

Rocks in the mantle do not act like normal rocks. If you were to hit them with a hammer, they would not break, but would squish, like Silly Putty squeezed in your hand. We are even closer to Earth's center now, so the temperature has risen to almost 2,000°F (1,093°C). The rocks are so warm that they are almost melting, and now they ooze like warm butter. This is the most important property of Earth—the property that allows all of Earth, with its mountains and volcanoes, to function.

For us, this means your jackhammer will not work. If you hammer into it, the rock will ooze right back, like trying to jack-hammer through mud. This rock acts like butter, so let's treat it like butter. Grab a butter knife and start carving. It is almost 2,000 miles (3,219 km) until we reach a new level.

As you carve down through Earth's mantle, you will notice something strange. The rocks here are green: neon, bright, lime green. They almost glow. This is a rock that geologists call peridotite, and it makes up almost the entire mantle of the Earth. It is neon green because it contains so much of the green mineral olivine.

As you carve your way down through this neon green mantle, you feel hotter and hotter. The temperature rises to more than 2,000°F (1,093°C). Then 3,000°F (1,649°C). Then 4,000°F (2,204°C). As you near Earth's core, the rocks become softer, like butter left too long in the sunlight. Your digging goes faster now through the soft rock.

When you reach the bottom of Earth's mantle, you are in for a surprise. As your butter knife cuts through the last of the neon green mantle, a geyser will erupt from the hole. This geyser is not made of hot water—it is made of dark gray, boiling liquid metal. This is the **outer core** of the planet: a 1,500-mile-deep (2,414 km) ocean of scalding-hot liquid metal. Jackhammers and knives will do you no good here, so pull on some heat-resistant scuba gear and dive in.

As you dive down toward the center of the planet, look around. The liquid metal is dark gray because it is made almost entirely of the elements iron and nickel. These are heavy elements, and swimming through them is difficult. It will feel like swimming through thick molasses: slow and sticky. You will find no rocks here. It is too hot for them to retain their solid structure. The temperature is approaching 5,000°F (2,760°C)—twice as hot as the flame from a blowtorch.

And then, suddenly, as you swim down, your hand will touch solid metal. This is Earth's **inner core**: a 1,400-mile-wide (2,253 km) ball of iron and nickel at the very center of the Earth. The core is more than 700 miles (1,127 km) deep, and all solid metal. Your swim fins are no use—you will need some TNT. Grab a few sticks and let's blast our way to the center.

As you blast down, you will notice the heat. This place is hotter than anything you have found so far: almost 6,000°F (3,516°C). You might wonder: If it is so hot, how can the core stay solid? Why doesn't it melt?

The answer is above you. Pressing down on top of the core are more than 3,000 miles (4,828 km) of rock and liquid metal. The weight is unbelievable. The moment the core starts to melt, the weight above presses down on all the atoms, smashing them back together into a solid.

If you had actually journeyed to the center of the Earth, you too would be crushed. Your bones would be crushed, and even the molecules that make up your bones would be crushed. This is called metamorphism. The molecules in your body—most of them containing the element carbon—would realign to a new structure that could bear the weight of the world pressing down on them. That new structure is diamond. If, instead of sitting there at your desk, you had dug a hole to the center of the Earth, you would have turned into one giant diamond.

THE BIRTH OF NEW ROCKS: CONVECTION AND THE MANTLE

Climb out of that hole. You have just passed through all the layers of the Earth: 20 miles (32 km) of pink granite crust; 2,000 miles (3,219 km) of green, butterlike mantle; 1,500 miles (2,414 km) of the liquid-iron outer core; and more than 700 miles (1,127 km) of the solid-metal inner core.

Together, these bizarre layers produce all the rocks on Earth through a process called **convection**.

The story of convection begins in the core: that blisteringly hot ball of metal nestled 3,000 miles (4,828 km) below you. Heat from the core rises up through the soft mantle, making the rocks even softer and lighter. Like warm air, warm rock rises. The hotter rocks near the core slowly ooze up through the mantle, joining with other upward-flowing rocks to make a giant, one-way highway flowing up toward the surface. When this highway hits the crust, it can go no further. It crashes against the bottom of the crust and flows sideways along its base. Here, near Earth's surface, the rocks are far from the hot core that made them soft like butter. As they cool, they become heavier. Eventually, they are too cold and heavy, and they sink back down toward the core. There, they are warmed and bubble up again. The rocks in the Earth's mantle will warm and rise, then sink and cool over and over. This is convection. The giant circle that the rocks trace as they go up and down is called a **convection cell**.

Convection is not a gentle cycle. Cells can be thousands of miles wide, dragging whole mountains' worth of hot mantle rocks up from the depths of the Earth and grinding them along the bottom of the crust. Sometimes, the cell pulls the crust along with it. And sometimes it rips the crust in half.

This is where volcanic rocks are born. Convection tears the crust at its weakest places—usually in the middle of the ocean, where the crust is only about 4 miles (6.4 km) thick. Hot, neon green mantle rocks surge up into the crack—and now something strange happens. The mantle rocks are boiling hot, and have only stayed solid because of the enormous pressure of the rocks above them, pushing them down. Suddenly, the pressure is gone. The mantle rocks melt and become magma: liquid rock below the surface of the Earth. The magma rises through the broken crust and erupts from volcanoes on the seafloor. This is the birth of the rock called basalt.

Basalt is one of the most important rocks on Earth, and also the most common. It is a black rock, made of the minerals olivine, pyroxene, and plagioclase. When the lava erupts onto the ocean floor, it touches the cold water and cools instantly. The minerals do not have time to grow large, so only tiny crystals make up the rock. In some basalts, the crystals are so small that you cannot see them. Geologists call this rock fine-grained. There are many kinds of fine-grained rocks, and most of them erupt from volcanoes, so they are called **volcanic igneous rocks**. (Remember that *igneous* means "from fire"—any rock that cools from magma or lava.)

Sometimes magma from the melting mantle will surge up into Earth's crust and get stuck. When this happens, the magma cools slowly. The molecules in the magma have time to settle down with each other and form large crystals. The minerals in these rocks are huge, so geologists call them coarse-grained. These rocks do not erupt onto the surface, but remain in the Earth, so geologists call them **intrusive igneous rocks** (because they have *intruded* the crust). If basalt-like magma gets stuck in the crust, it forms the intrusive rock gabbro.

THE LIFE AND DEATH OF BASALT

Now you know how basalt and gabbro are made: draw heat from the core, stir up the mantle, and rip apart the crust. Voilà! But basalt's story does not end there. In fact, this is only the beginning. Let's follow a piece of basalt for a few hundred million years and see where it ends up.

The basalt forms, fine-grained and dark, at a deep undersea volcano where convection is tearing the crust open. This could be any ocean. Convection cells have ripped apart all of Earth's oceans, creating zigzagging cracks where basalt erupts from beneath. These cracks are called **spreading centers**, and our basalt will not stay there for long.

As more and more basalt erupts from the crack, it pushes the old basalt away, like a conveyor belt. Our basalt moves slowly away from the spreading center, pushed out by the new rocks. It is not just rocks: the entire crust of the ocean—a 4-mile-thick (6.4 km) slab called a **plate**—is being pushed away from the spreading center. This is the beginning of a process that geologists call **plate tectonics**: the slow movement of rocks across Earth's surface, pushed by the convection cells that are always transforming Earth from below.

Eventually, our basalt will reach the edge of the ocean: a continent. Continental crust is much thicker than oceanic crust. It is also lighter, since it is made of the rock granite, a much lighter rock than basalt. When our basalt and its plate reach the edge of a continent, they can go no further. Behind them, the spreading center is pushing more new rocks out, shoving them against the edge of the continent. With nowhere to go, our basalt and

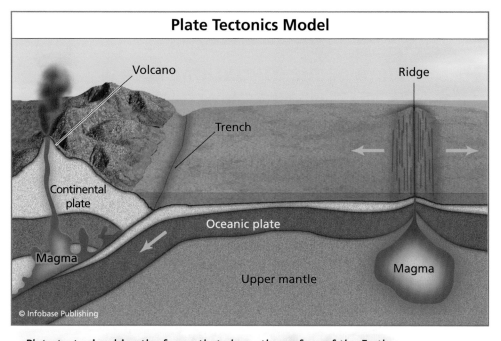

Plate tectonics drive the forces that shape the surface of the Earth, which leads to the constant transformation of rocks as the crust changes shape.

the entire plate it sits on can only do one thing: dive beneath the continent. Geologists call this a **subduction** zone. Here, our basalt will change. With its entire slab of fellow basaltic rocks, it will sink down, pushed beneath the continent.

The process does not go smoothly. The basalt is thrust violently beneath the continent and catches and breaks as it is ground between two walls of rock. The entire oceanic plate goes down, cracking and bending. When it breaks, it sends shock waves through the entire crust, producing earthquakes at the surface. This is why Japan experiences so many earthquakes: A slab of oceanic crust is subducting below it.

As it sinks back into the Earth, our piece of basalt heats up. Sometimes, the rocks become so hot that they melt. Our basalt is gone now—dragged down into the Earth's center, or melted again into magma. But its story is still not over, for magma does not sit still. It has to go somewhere, and turn into something else.

BIRTH OF THE CONTINENTAL ROCK

The magma rises, but it does not rise alone. Before subduction, our basalt had been underwater. It was soaked in water, mud, bits of kelp, and other ocean debris. When our basalt melts, so does the rest of this junk. Together, this watery, muddy magma rises up, away from the subducting oceanic plate and toward the overlying continent.

The magma bubbles up against the bottom of the continent. If the crust is thin there, the magma can punch straight through and erupt onto Earth's surface. These are not the unseen, underwater eruptions that ooze basalt into the ocean. They are often violent and catastrophic. The water trapped in the magma turns to steam and explodes out of the volcano, spraying molten rock and ash high into the air. This is called **explosive volcanism**, and it produces a very different kind of rock, called andesite.

Andesite is a volcanic rock, like basalt. It is made by melting basalt, mixing in some mud and water, then cooling the magma fast, forcing tiny crystals to form. The mud adds quartz and other minerals to the magma, so andesite is much richer in these minerals than basalt.

The quartz and other mud-minerals make andesite lighter than basalt—and much thicker. When it erupts at volcanoes, it does not flow, but it turns into sticky globs. It cannot go far. So, instead of growing sideways like the fat underwater volcanoes, an andesite volcano grows taller. This is why many of Earth's volcanoes are so high: They erupt andesite, which does not like to flow.

Our basalt has turned into something totally different: a quartz-rich andesite atop a high volcano. It might be sitting atop a volcano in the Andes mountains of South America, where a subducting ocean plate is melting and pumping andesitic lava up into volcanoes. Or perhaps it is sitting atop a volcano near Seattle, Washington, where explosive andesitic lavas cause such disasters as the Mount St. Helens eruption of 1980.

Regardless of where our andesite is sitting, its story is still not over yet.

THE TRANSFORMATION OF CONTINENTAL ROCK

Our rock was born in the sea, dragged beneath a continent and melted; then it bubbled up, exploded from a volcano, and now sits atop a continent, far from the pushing and pulling of the ocean plates. But it has not escaped the process of plate tectonics.

As the mantle bubbles up at spreading centers, it pushes the ocean plates away. Sometimes a continent will ride along with the ocean plate, moving away from the spreading center. North America is doing this right now: riding with the Atlantic Ocean westward toward Japan. Geologists call the motion of the continents around the world **continental drift.**

All ocean plates are headed toward a subduction zone, which means the continents are doing the same. But, unlike the thin ocean crust, continental crust cannot be pushed down into a subduction zone because it is too thick. Whenever a continent gets sucked into a subduction zone, it mashes up against the other overlying continent, producing what geologists call a **continental collision**.

Continental collisions build mountains. The two continents grind into each other slowly—moving only a few inches every year for millions of years. As they merge, they squeeze their rocks up into colossal mountains. This is how Mount Everest formed: The slab of continental crust that carries India plowed into the edge of Asia. The slow merging of these two pieces of crust is squeezing Mount Everest—and the rest of the Himalayas—to a higher altitude every year.

Our andesite, sitting on top of its volcano, is headed for this fate. Maybe in 2 million years, maybe in 200 million, a slab of continental crust will come riding toward that subduction zone, get jammed, and plow straight into our andesite and the continent on which it sits.

The collision will be fatal for the andesite, and for most of the rocks involved. Under the extreme heat and pressure of the collision, the minerals in our andesite will rearrange themselves, metamorphosing into new minerals that can withstand the high temperatures and pressures. Geologists call the new rock that forms a metamorphic rock.

Every rock is different and so it will change into a different metamorphic rock when exposed to different levels of heat and pressure. If we had smashed our basalt between two continents, it would have transformed into what geologists call a greenschist, then an eclogite, then a blueschist. If we had heated our basalt just right, it might have turned into an amphibolite or granulite. These are all types of metamorphic rocks that form when you heat or push on basalt.

Our andesite has similar minerals as does our basalt, so it will probably form a similar metamorphic rock. Perhaps the collision only heated our andesite to, say, 800°F (427°C) and crushed it under only 4 miles (6.4 km) of rock. If so, the minerals in our andesite (quartz, plagioclase, pyroxene, and olivine) might dissolve and rearrange themselves into the metamorphic minerals chlorite, actinolite, albite, and epidote. These minerals are distinctly green, so our rock would turn green, too, and would now be what geologists call a greenschist. We will talk more about metamorphic rocks in Chapter 5. For now, we still have our rock to follow.

WIND, RAIN, AND TIME

Our basalt melted, erupted, and became an andesite. Our andesite was smashed between two colliding continents and became a greenschist. And still, the rock is not done with its journey.

Our greenschist was born in the heart of a tremendous mountain chain. It will sit there for millions of years, deep inside a mountain that is pushed higher and higher by the ongoing collision of two continents happening all around it. Outside, there will be snow, ice, wind, rain, and avalanches, but none of these elements will touch our greenschist—at least not yet.

Snow, ice, wind, and rain slowly chip away at rocks. The wind blows off tiny bits (which are called **grains**) and blasts them into other rocks, which chips off more tiny grains. The snow freezes the rock, causing it to crack open. The rain washes these grains away, exposing new rock to be sandblasted by the wind and frozen by the snow. Geologists call this constant beating **weathering** or **erosion**.

As the colliding continents push our greenschist's mountain higher, wind, rain, and snow grind it down. Eventually, after thousands of years, they will grind down all the rock overlying our greenschist, and the greenschist itself will again be on the surface of the Earth. There, wind, rain, and snow will begin to grind it down, too. This is the end of our greenschist—but not of our rock's story.

STREAMS TO THE RIVER, RIVERS TO THE SEA

Weathering has reduced the greenschist to tiny specks of sand. Next, rain and melting snow will carry the sand down the mountain. In mountain streams, the grains will join other grains, weathered off the mountain in the same way. The streams will

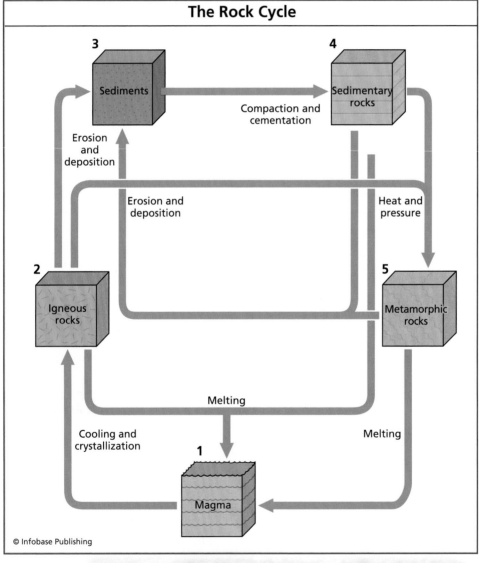

The Rock Cycle

3 Sediments

4 Sedimentary rocks

Compaction and cementation

Erosion and deposition

Erosion and deposition

Heat and pressure

2 Igneous rocks

5 Metamorphic rocks

Melting

Cooling and crystallization

Melting

1 Magma

© Infobase Publishing

The rock cycle describes how rocks are processed through geological processes over long periods of time.

The Case of the Echoing Earth

No one has ever been to the center of the Earth. No one has even dug as deep as the mantle. Geologists can only infer Earth's internal structure using **seismic waves**—pulses of high pressure that start in an earthquake and radiate down through the Earth's interior.

Geologists focus on two kinds of seismic waves: pressure waves (called P-waves) and shear waves (S-waves). Pressure waves are much like sound waves. They move through material by pressing together and stretching apart the molecules that they touch. Shear waves are more like ocean waves, moving in S-shaped curves through a material. These waves are subtly different. Imagine a man standing in a glass box on the beach. The ocean waves (S-waves) would not be able to reach him—they are stopped by the glass barrier. However, if the glass was thin, he might be able to hear sound waves (P-waves) from the outside. Like sound, P-waves can move through some barriers; like ocean waves, S-waves cannot.

This subtle distinction is what allows geologists to "see" inside the Earth. For example, an earthquake in Japan might produce both P- and S-waves, which echo through the Earth. When S-waves hit a barrier—for example, a liquid inner core—they stop. P-waves can make it through, though they might be distorted. Geologists around the world can then detect which waves make it all the way through the Earth and how they have been altered along the way. By measuring billions of P- and S-waves from billions of earthquakes, seismologists have been able to infer the depth and composition of each of Earth's internal layers. The technique is so strange and difficult to master that many geologists refer to seismology as geology's "black art."

carry these to larger rivers, which will carry them all down the length of their route through the continent and to the sea.

As the river merges with the ocean, it slows down and stops flowing. All the energy it had flowing downhill is lost. It can no longer push along grains of sand, so the sands stop where they are and settle to the bottom of the ocean. Smaller sand grains are lighter and so they settle out later. Sometimes the smallest sand grains are carried far away from the coast. These settle to the bottom of the ocean to make mud: a goo of water and very fine-grained bits of rock that have been chipped off nearby mountains. If buried beneath enough sediment, the mud may **compact**, or squeeze down, to make a new rock called mudstone. Mudstones are one kind of sedimentary rock, meaning rocks that are made from sediments.

Our rock has returned to the ocean, shattered into a billion tiny bits. But its story is not over. Sitting atop the basaltic ocean crust, our rock is still moving with plate tectonics. One day, it will run into a continent again and be pushed down into another sub-duction zone. With the basalt beneath it, it will melt, bubble up, and explode from another volcano as a new andesite. It will sit again at the top of some continent until it is crushed in another continental collision, or weathered away by wind, rain, and time into sand and swept out again to the sea. Our rock—and every other rock on Earth, including all the ones beneath you right now—will go through this cycle over and over again, forever. This geologic merry-go-round is what geologists call the **rock cycle**.

For some rocks, the rock cycle does end—at least, temporar-ily. Sometimes, a rock will be smashed beneath a continent in a subduction zone, and, instead of melting, it will just keep sink-ing. These sinking rocks move slowly down into the mantle, back toward the liquid outer core. Geologists do not know what hap-pens next. Maybe they rejoin the mantle. Maybe they stay in soft, immobile slabs of ocean crust, buried at the center of the Earth, until some passing warm convection cell spirits them upward to erupt in another ocean and start life as a basalt once again.

5

Collecting Rocks:
WHAT IS IT AND HOW DID IT GET HERE?

▲ ▲ ▲

WE UNDERSTAND SO MUCH ABOUT THE EARTH NOWADAYS. WE understand what rocks are made of, how they form, and how to identify their minerals. But if you picked up a random rock in your front yard, would you know where it came from or how it formed? To truly understand the Earth, we need to be able to decipher the individual rocks that we find.

To do this, we need a rock from every part of the Earth—the ocean bottoms, the hearts of mountains, subduction zones, volcanoes—everything. We need to know their story: how each rock was born and how it changed over time. This is the key to a rock collection: discovering the story behind every rock.

You can start by going outside and picking up a rock. Any rock will do, to start with. You can figure out the life story of your rock by examining it. The first step is to decide what kind of rock it is.

HOW TO IDENTIFY ROCK TYPES

Rocks are given names based on how they formed and what minerals they contain. For example, geologists call a volcanic rock made of the minerals plagioclase, olivine, and pyroxene a basalt. If you took a basalt and somehow mixed in some quartz, you would have to call the rock andesite. The first step in giving a rock a name is to figure out how it formed: Is it sedimentary, metamorphic, or igneous?

Is It a Sedimentary Rock?

Sedimentary rocks are usually easy to identify. These rocks are made from sediment—the sand, dust, and mud that gets chipped off mountains—so they usually look familiar to you: A sandstone looks like a big ball of hardened sand; a mudstone looks like a ball of dry mud; a conglomerate looks like a bunch of pebbles glued together.

Even if your rock does not look like a ball of sand or mud, you might still have a sedimentary rock. Sedimentary rocks—like the mudstone that formed at the end of Chapter 4—usually look striped. Most sediments are laid down flat on the bottom of an ocean or lake. Then more are laid down on top, then more, and so on, until the rock looks like a layered cake. If your rock has these kinds of straight stripes, you can call it **layered**. It is probably a sedimentary rock. (Some sedimentary rocks do not look like sand or mud and sometimes they do not have layers. We will talk about those later in this chapter.)

If your rock has stripes that are *not* straight—if the stripes bend and swirl across the rock—then it is not a sedimentary rock. When rocks are crushed and transformed into metamorphic rocks, they sometimes develop these beautiful swirling, twisting stripes. These are called **foliations**, and they indicate if you have a metamorphic rock.

Is It a Metamorphic Rock?

Metamorphic rocks are usually easy to identify because they are so beautiful. They tend to be made of sparkly minerals like mica, andalusite, and sillimanite. Some have giant crystals of soccer ball–shaped garnet and staurolites, which are shaped like crosses.

In metamorphic rocks called schists, the minerals look stretched, almost as if they are all marching in rows in one direction. Geologists call this pattern a **schistosity**—the hallmark of a schist.

In another metamorphic rock, called gneiss (pronounced "nice"), the minerals have all grouped together to form bands: one band of quartz, then another of biotite, with globs of garnet crystals scattered throughout. You can almost always identify a gneiss by these beautiful, crystal-filled bands.

Earth has many more kinds of metamorphic rocks, which we will discuss below. For now, if your rock is sparkly or swirly, it might be metamorphic.

Is It an Igneous Rock?

If your rock is neither sedimentary nor metamorphic, then it is igneous: a rock made by melting other rocks into magma or lava. Igneous rocks can be difficult to identify. Volcanic igneous rocks, which explode from volcanoes, have minerals that are too tiny to see. Intrusive igneous rocks, which cool slowly underground, have larger minerals, but can still be tough to identify. We will start with color.

A rock's color is not random. A black rock is dark because it is made of dark minerals. A pink rock is made of pink minerals. A striped rock is made of dark minerals in dark stripes and light minerals in light stripes. A rock's color is telling you what it is made of.

Dark rocks tend to be made of minerals with lots of the elements magnesium and iron. For example, the minerals olivine and pyroxene, which are both very dark minerals, are rich in magnesium and iron atoms. For this reason, geologists tend to call dark rocks **mafic** ("ma" from *magnesium* and "fic" from the Latin word for *iron*). The volcanic igneous rock basalt is a mafic rock.

Light-colored rocks tend to be made of the minerals feldspar and quartz, which are both rich in the element silicon. Geologists call these rocks **felsic** ("fel" from *feldspar* and "sic" from *silicon*). The intrusive igneous rock granite is a felsic rock.

Rocks that are somewhere between light and dark are called **intermediate** rocks and can have mafic minerals, or felsic minerals like feldspar and quartz. The volcanic igneous rock andesite is an intermediate rock.

MINERAL SIZE

The next thing to observe about your rock is how big the minerals are. If the minerals in your rock are too small to see, then your rock is fine-grained and probably erupted from a volcano. If you can see the minerals, but they are small, then your rock is medium-grained. (It still probably erupted from a volcano.) If the minerals are large and easy to see, then your rock is coarse-grained and probably cooled slowly underground. Sometimes the minerals are as big as your thumb—or bigger!—and the rock is called very coarse-grained.

Write down whether your rock is fine-grained, medium-grained, coarse-grained, or very coarse grained. If you can see the minerals, try to identify them, using the skills you learned in Chapters 2 and 3. Write down what minerals you see. Now compare your description of the rock to the rock descriptions below.

THE USUAL SUSPECTS

Earth is made of hundreds of different kinds of rocks, but most of them are rarely found on the surface. Usually, you will run into only a handful of types. Here is a quick guide to identifying the usual suspects.

Basalt

Basalt is one of the most common rocks on Earth, making up most of the ocean crust.

Rock Type: Volcanic (igneous).
Minerals: Basalt is a rock made of the minerals olivine, pyroxene, and plagioclase.

Color: Mafic (dark gray to black). Basalt is rich in the mineral pyroxene, which is made of the atoms silicon, oxygen, and either iron or magnesium.

Grain Size: Very fine-grained to medium-grained. Basalt is a volcanic igneous rock: It erupts from volcanoes. When it does, the lava touches air or water and cools fast, leaving the minerals almost no time to form. The grains are small—sometimes so small you cannot see them.

Other Identifying Information: Basalt often erupts from volcanoes, but that can take a while. Sometimes, the liquid basalt lava sits underneath the volcano, waiting to erupt, for years. While it is there, bubbling away, it starts to cool and form minerals. When it finally does erupt, all the other minerals will form quickly, making small grains—but the minerals that cooled slowly underground will be big. Geologists call this a **porphyritic texture**: little dots of large minerals in a basalt. Sometimes the white mineral plagioclase forms the big crystals, and the dark rock looks polka-dotted. Sometimes the mineral olivine forms the big crystals, and the rock looks like it is covered with translucent green raisins. Not every basalt will look like this, but, if you find one that does, then you know that it had to wait beneath a volcano for a long time before it could erupt!

Sometimes, you will find basalts that are full of tiny holes. These are places where air bubbles were trapped in the magma and escaped. Geologists call this a **vesicular texture**. Only volcanic rocks have a vesicular texture.

Where It Is Found: The entire ocean floor is made of basalt. Almost every island with volcanoes is made of basalt, too: for example, Hawaii, the Galápagos Islands, and Iceland. Sometimes basalt can erupt onto continents, as well. If convection cells rip open a weak part of a continent, then basalt will flow up from the mantle and erupt onto land. Huge portions of Idaho, Montana, Washington, and Oregon are covered with basalt flows that erupted when the continental crust cracked open to reveal the mantle

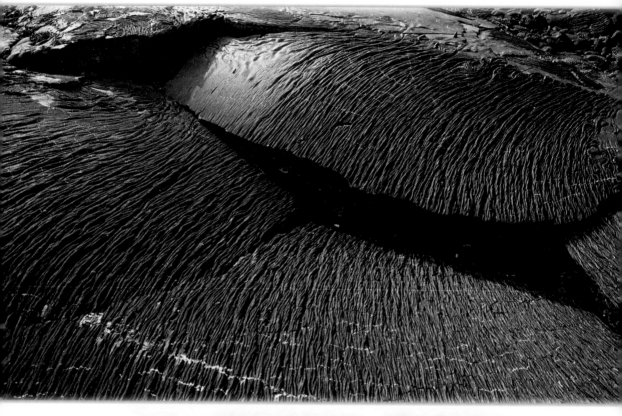

These lava plates in the Galapagos Islands are made of basalt.

below. If you find basalt, remember that the crust of the Earth had to open for that rock to form. That you found it means the rock was brought there from a volcanically-active area, or the crust has cracked open nearby.

Gabbro

Gabbro is basalt's cousin. When basalt lava gets stuck underground, it cools slowly to make huge minerals. The result is gabbro.

Rock Type: Intrusive (igneous).
Minerals: Like basalt, gabbro is a rock made of the minerals olivine, pyroxene, and plagioclase.

Color: Mafic (dark gray to black).

Grain Size: Medium-grained to coarse-grained.

Other Identifying Information: Gabbro's dark color and big minerals make it easy to spot. Oftentimes, the pyroxene crystals are so large that they make the rock shimmer slightly, like black sequins. Gabbro will not have a porphyritic or vesicular texture, because it cools slowly underground.

Where It is Found: The entire ocean floor is made of basalt, but the basalt underneath the ocean's floor that never made it to the surface is called gabbro. Sometimes basaltic lava gets stuck in continental crust, as well, and forms gabbro. The overlying rock must be eroded away before the gabbro reaches the surface. If you find a gabbro, you know it either came from inside the ocean crust, or from deep underground.

Gabbro

Andesite

Andesite is similar to basalt. It is a volcanic igneous rock, erupting from volcanoes on land instead of in the sea.

Rock Type: Volcanic (igneous).

Minerals: Like basalt, andesite is rich in plagioclase and pyroxene. But, since it mixed with melted mud, it has many more minerals: quartz, biotite, and hornblende, for example.

Color: Intermediate to felsic (dark gray to light tan). Because andesite has more light-colored minerals (like quartz and feldspar), it looks lighter than basalt.

Grain Size: Fine-grained to medium-grained. Andesite lava erupts from volcanoes and cools quickly, giving its minerals little chance to grow large. The minerals in andesite are usually too small to see.

Other Identifying Information: Like basalt, andesite often has a porphyritic texture. This is caused by the big globs of minerals that cooled slowly underground while the lava was waiting to erupt from the volcano. The mineral that cools fastest is often the white plagioclase, making rocks that have large white flakes all over them. If you find such an andesite, then you know it had to wait underground to erupt. Andesite can also have a bubbly or vesicular texture, meaning it was full of gas bubbles that escaped when the lava erupted.

Where It is Found: We followed the birth of an andesite rock in Chapter 4. Andesite forms at the edge of a subduction zone, when an ocean plate is shoved beneath a continent and melts. The melted basalt mixes with melted mud, bubbles up, and erupts from enormous volcanoes on the edge of the continent. If you are looking for andesite, then you should look at the edges of continents, where ocean plates are subducting beneath them. In North America, you would look in the Pacific Northwest. An

Andesite

ocean plate is subducting beneath Washington, Oregon, and Idaho, producing enormous mountains, rich in andesite. If you were in South America, you would find andesite in the Andes mountains—the mountains that the mineral was name after.

The Case of the Martian "Andesite"

Mars, the next planet out from the Sun, does not have plate tectonics. Its rocks do not subduct, melt, re-erupt, and crush together to form mountains—they just sit there. So, when a team of planetary geologists announced in 1998 that they had found the rock andesite on Mars, the geology community was deeply confused.

Andesite is a volcanic rock that forms when basalt subducts below a continent, melts, mixes with mud and water, and re-erupts in violent explosions. Mars has no subduction, no continents, no water, and no violent explosions—yet, almost half the planet appears to be made of andesite!

Planetary geologists still do not understand why andesite should occur on Mars. Some think that these andesites are, in fact, basalts that were melted and remelted many times before they erupted onto the surface. And many question whether these rocks even *are* andesite—they might instead be basalts that were subtly altered by water to make them look andesitic. Learning the origin of these rocks will dramatically impact our understanding of how Mars works, but more than a decade after their discovery, geologists are no closer to understanding how they formed.

Rhyolite

Rhyolite is similar to andesite. It is a volcanic igneous rock that erupts from volcanoes on land. Like andesite, it forms on the edges of continents where melted ocean crust bubbles up from subduction zones. Unlike andesite, though, rhyolite is much richer in quartz.

Rock Type: Volcanic (igneous).

Minerals: Rhyolite has lots of quartz and feldspar. Sometimes that is all it has, and it looks like a big chunk of pink and clear crystals. Some rhyolites also have tiny black flecks of biotite, hornblende, or magnetite.

Color: Felsic (light gray to light pink). Rhyolite is usually so rich in the pink mineral feldspar that it looks a little pink itself.

Grain Size: Fine-grained. Rhyolite is a volcanic igneous rock. It erupts as magma from a volcano and cools fast when it touches the air. It cools so quickly, the minerals form tiny grains that are barely visible.

Other Identifying Information: Like basalt, rhyolite often has a porphyritic texture: big globs of minerals that cooled slowly underground while the lava was waiting

Rhyolite

to erupt from the volcano. The mineral that cools fastest in rhyolite is often the pink feldspar. If you find such a rhyolite, then you know it had to wait underground to erupt. Rhyolite can also have a vesicular texture, if it was full of gas bubbles that escaped when the lava erupted.

Where It is Found: Like andesite, rhyolite forms when ocean crust is sucked below a continent in a subduction zone where it melts with mud and water, bubbles up to the surface, and erupts from volcanoes on continents. You will find lots of rhyolite in the western half of North America—for example, in Nevada, Utah, and Arizona.

Rhyolites are fascinating rocks because of how they form. Remember that rhyolite is made of melted ocean crust, mixed with mud and water. Most rhyolites are mixed with so much water that when they erupt, they explode. Instead of a smooth flow of gentle lava cascading down a volcano, the rhyolite rains down as boiling-hot bits of ash, covering the surrounding countryside in molten rock. These explosions kill everything in their path. But rhyolite is not as common as andesite. Rhyolite is rich in the minerals quartz and feldspar: two strong minerals that cool quickly and do not like to flow. As a result, rhyolite is a very **viscous** lava, meaning it moves more like molasses than water. In fact, it is so viscous that it usually gets stuck underground instead of erupting on the surface. When this happens, the rhyolite magma cools slowly and forms the intrusive igneous rock called granite.

Granite

Rock Type: Intrusive (igneous).
Minerals: Granite has the same minerals as rhyolite.
Color: Felsic (light gray to light pink).
Grain Size: Coarse-grained to very coarse-grained.

Other Identifying Information: Polished granite makes a beautiful building stone and is often used to make banks and office buildings.

Where It is Found: Like rhyolite, granite forms when ocean crust is sucked below a continent in a subduction zone, melted with mud and water, and bubbled up into the overlying continent. Unlike rhyolite, though, granite never erupts onto the surface—it cools slowly under-

Granite

ground. Eventually, the hardened granite is pushed up to the surface to become a mountain. If your rock is a granite, this is probably where you found it—most mountains in western North America are made of granite.

Sandstone

Rock Type: Sedimentary.

Minerals: Sandstones are made of sand. If the sand formed from granite, then the sandstone has all the minerals of granite. If the sand formed from basalt, then the sandstone has all the minerals of basalt. Most sandstones you find will be made almost entirely of quartz, though, because other minerals break down too quickly into smaller grains before they can form sandstone.

Sandstone

Color: Sandstones can be any color, but are usually tan to pink.

Grain Size: You can usually see the individual sand grains. If the grains are too small to see, then you probably have a mudstone.

Other Identifying Information: Sandstones are sedimentary rocks, so you will often see layers in them. Since they form in streambeds, you may also often find fossils of the ancient animals that lived on the bottoms of the streams.

Where It is Found: Sandstones are found all over North America—anywhere that a shallow lake or stream might have passed. They tend not to form in deep water, since they require a lot of sand, and sand usually accumulates in shallow water and beaches. Some particularly beautiful red sandstones are found in northern Arizona.

Mudstone/Shale

Mudstone and shale are similar rocks. Mudstone is usually softer than shale, but they are both made of mud.

Rock Type: Sedimentary.

Minerals: Like sandstone, mudstones can be made of many minerals. The minerals are usually too tiny to see, though, since they are inside the tiny flecks that made the mud.

Color: Mudstones can be any color, but are usually dark brown to black.

Grain Size: Tiny. Mudstones are made of mud, which is made of extremely tiny bits of dust mixed with water.

Other Identifying Information: If you can break the rock apart in your hand, you call it mudstone. If it is too hard to break apart, then you call it shale.

Where It is Found: Like sandstone, mudstones are found anywhere there is or once was water. They tend to form in deeper water, like in the bottoms of lakes and deep rivers.

Mudstone

Conglomerate

Rock Type: Sedimentary.

Minerals: Anything and everything! Conglomerates are made of lots of huge pebbles that got smashed together into a rock. When you look at a conglomerate, you can usually see little mashed-up pebbles of granites, basalts, sandstones, other conglomerates, or any other rock that was in the area when it formed.

Color: Conglomerates can be any color—it depends on what color pebbles it has.

Grain Size: Conglomerates can be made of small pebbles or giant boulders.

Other Identifying Information: Conglomerates look polka-dotted, with giant, multicolored pebbles for dots and mud or sand in between that holds them together like glue.

Where It is Found: Conglomerates usually form in places with lots of pebbles, like fast rivers and avalanches. You can find them all over North America, but they are rarer than sandstones or mudstones.

Conglomerate rock

Limestone

A limestone is a curious sort of sedimentary rock. It is not actually made of sediments worn away from other rocks. Limestone forms in the ocean where microscopic animals make shells out of the mineral calcite. When the animals die, their shells settle onto the seafloor. When enough shells pile up and are buried, they press together to form limestone.

>*Rock Type:* Sedimentary.
>*Minerals:* Calcite (tiny animal shells).
>*Color:* Light tan to pink.
>*Grain Size:* Usually very fine-grained.
>*Other Identifying Information:* Usually, the animal shells are microscopic, but sometimes they are large enough to see. When you can see the animal shells, the rock is called **fossiliferous** limestone, meaning "fossil-rich."
>*Where It is Found:* Limestone forms in very deep oceans where microscopic animals live. Long ago, much of North America was under a deep ocean, which is why huge areas of the Midwest are covered with limestone. Kansas, Illinois, Missouri, Iowa, and Indiana all have beautiful limestones made of ancient microscopic shells.

Slate

Slate is a metamorphic rock that forms from mudstone or shale.

>*Rock Type:* Metamorphic.
>*Minerals:* Slate usually has mica and chlorite, but they are usually too small to see.
>*Color:* Dark gray to black.
>*Grain Size:* Tiny. This is a rock made by smashing lots of mud together, then smashing it some more.
>*Other Identifying Information:* The best way to identify slate is by noticing how it breaks. Slate breaks into long, thin sheets, like paper. These sheets are so smooth and perfect that they are often made into roofs for houses or sidewalk stones.

Gray slate

Where It is Found: Slate forms when mudstones are pushed
together in a continental collision, so they are usually
found on mountains. The Appalachian Mountains on
the east coast of North America are bristling with slate.

Schist

Schist is a metamorphic rock that forms from either sedimentary
rocks or volcanic rocks. Oftentimes, a mudstone will turn into a
slate, and, if the continental collision continues and the heat and

pressure continue to rise, the slate will transform even further into a schist.

Rock Type: Metamorphic.

Minerals: Schists usually contain mica and chlorite, but they are usually too small to see. A schist that formed in a particularly violent continental collision, with higher heats and pressures, might have the minerals garnet, staurolite, or kyanite, as well. If you see these minerals, you know that the schist formed at high temperatures.

Color: Schists are usually dark, but can look silvery if they contain muscovite.

Grain Size: Usually small, but it is easy to see specific minerals.

Other Identifying Information: In a schist, all the minerals line up. If you can see the paperlike flakes of muscovite, they should all line up like pages of a book. This is called schistosity.

Schist

Where It is Found: Schists form in continental collisions, especially ones that involve mudstones. They cover the Appalachians along the east coast of North America.

Gneiss

Gneiss (pronounced "nice") is a metamorphic rock that forms when another rock—usually a sedimentary or metamorphic rock—is heated almost to the point of melting.

Rock Type: Metamorphic.
Minerals: Feldspar, quartz, hornblende, and biotite. Sometimes tiny garnets or staurolites form, as well.

Gneiss

Color: Gneisses are striped, with swirling bands of all different colors.

Grain Size: Gneisses can have huge minerals or tiny ones—or a mixture of both. Usually, you will be able to see the individual minerals—all different colors and shapes. Gneiss is a beautiful rock.

Other Identifying Information: Gneisses are striped—that is what defines a gneiss. The minerals have been so smashed by the pressure of the continental collision that they have separated: one type of mineral into one layer, another type into another layer, and so on.

Where It is Found: Gneisses form deep in the bellies of mountains during continental collisions. They require extreme heat and pressure to form, and so usually only form in the most intense mountain-building events. In North America, gneisses are found in the Appalachians and other old mountains.

Amphibolite

Amphibolite is a metamorphic rock that forms from basalt or gabbro.

Rock Type: Metamorphic.

Minerals: Hornblende, plagioclase, and mica.

Color: Dark green to black.

Grain Size: Usually fine-grained, but sometimes you can see large minerals.

Other Identifying Information: Amphibolites are made almost entirely of the dark green mineral hornblende (which belongs to the amphibole family of minerals).

Where It is Found: Amphibolites usually form from basalt, so they usually form in the ocean. When basalt is smashed down into a subduction zone, it heats up, and the parts that do not melt turn into amphibolite. Geologists are not sure how amphibolites make their way from deep in a subduction zone onto the continents where they are found.

Amphibolite

Marble

Marble is a metamorphic rock that forms from limestone.

Rock Type: Metamorphic.

Minerals: Pure marble only has calcite in it, since pure limestone is only made of the mineral calcite. But most marbles are "dirty marbles" and have bits of other minerals in them, too: black pyroxenes, red garnets, and dark green amphiboles.

Color: Tan or white to pink.

Grain Size: Tiny. You usually cannot see the minerals in a marble.

Where It is Found: Marbles are usually found in long bands, smashed between layers of other metamorphic rocks, like slates and schists. A long belt of marble runs through Maine and Vermont.

Above, one can see the difference made by the metamorphosis of limestone *(left)* into marble *(right)*.

BUILDING A COLLECTION

Congratulations! You have identified your rock. Now add it to your collection by making a label for it.

Your rock's label should tell you everything about the rock. Write down the rock's name (basalt, granite, marble, etc.), where you found it, what color it is, and what size the grains are. Can you make out any minerals? Does the rock have a porphyritic texture? If so, what mineral makes up the polka dots? Based on where you found the rock, how do you think it formed: at a spreading center, from ocean volcanoes like Hawaii, in a lake, or in a mountain collision? Write all this down on your rock's label. Try to write out a story, describing where the rock formed and what happened to it afterward. Cite your evidence—why do you think your story is true?

Look for rocks wherever you go. If you take a family vacation, you will see them alongside the road. When you stop, pick them up and look at them—how are they different from the rocks you find at home? Why do you think that is? Was this area once underwater? Did the crust rip open and pour out basalt? Are there volcanoes with rhyolite nearby? Everywhere you go now, you can interpret the ground beneath your feet—simply by looking at the rocks you see around you. Congratulations—that's geology!

Glossary

▲

Acicular   A habit in which a mineral's crystals are long, thin, and needle-like.

Aggregate   A habit in which a mineral's crystals are bunched together.

Alkaline   A slightly metallic taste that some minerals have.

Amorphous A habit in which a mineral does not have any specific structure at all. Most amorphous minerals have a melted appearance.

Andesite   A volcanic igneous rock made mostly of the minerals plagioclase and pyroxene, but sometimes containing some quartz, biotite, and hornblende. Andesite usually erupts from volcanoes along the edges of subduction zones.

Atom   The universe's building block. There are more than 100 different kinds of atoms—called elements—and they make up everything in the universe. Atoms hook together to form molecules, which then stack to make minerals.

Basalt   A volcanic igneous rock made mostly of the minerals plagioclase, pyroxene, and olivine. Basalt is one of the most common rocks on Earth: It makes up most of the ocean crust.

Bladed   A habit in which a mineral's crystals are long and flat with a pointed end.

Blocky   A habit in which a rock or mineral is shaped like a pile of boxes.

Bond The "glue" that holds molecules together. Atoms bond together to form molecules, which stack to form minerals.

Botryoidal A habit in which a rock or mineral is shaped like a bunch of grapes.

Cleavage The way a mineral breaks. Minerals are made of molecules that are stacked in a certain way. The way the molecules are stacked determines how the mineral will break. For example, the mineral mica stacks in flat sheets of molecules, so the cleavage is "plate-like."

Columnar A habit in which crystals are shaped like columns.

Compact The act of squishing sediments together to form a rock. If sand, mud, or any other sediment is buried under enough material, it will compact to form a rock.

Conchoidal fracture One way that a mineral can break, forming a smooth, curving surface like the inside of a clamshell. Quartz is famous for its conchoidal fracture.

Continent A large piece of land sitting above the ocean. Today, Earth has seven continents: Africa, Antarctica, Asia, Australia, Europe, North America, and South America. In the past, Earth has had as few as one and as many as a dozen continents because they move around (see continental drift).

Continental collision The collision of two or more continents due to plate tectonics. Continental collisions squish rocks and push up mountain ranges.

Continental crust The rocks that make up continents. Continental crust is usually granite, with a few other rocks here and there. The continental crust is usually about 20 miles (about 32 km) thick, compared to the approximately 4-mile-thick (about 6.4 km) oceanic crust.

Continental drift The slow movement of continents across Earth's surface. As new oceanic crust erupts from spreading centers in the middle of the oceans, Earth's continents are pushed around. They move slowly—just a few inches every year—but over millions of years, this adds up to millions of miles.

Convection The slow rising of hot mantle material toward Earth's surface and the slow sinking of cool mantle material toward Earth's core. Convection powers plate tectonics, bringing hot magma up from inside the Earth to erupt on the surface and dragging cold slabs of ocean crust back down into the hot interior of the Earth along subduction zones.

Convection cell A circle of heat transfer formed in the mantle: Hot rocks rise on one side of the circle until they hit the crust. There, they either split the crust and erupt onto the surface, or cool and fall back down the other side of the circle. This is the same motion as a lava lamp, and it powers plate tectonics.

Core The center of Earth. The core has two parts: the outer core, which is made of boiling-hot liquid iron; and the inner core, which is made of scalding-hot solid iron and nickel. Earth's heat comes from its core.

Crust The "skin" of the Earth. The crust is a thick layer of rock that sits on top of the mantle, covering the entire surface of the Earth. Earth has two kinds of crust: continental crust, which is thick and made of granite; and oceanic crust, which is thin and made of basalt.

Crystal A well-formed mineral. Crystals usually have flat sides and an obviously geometric shape, as opposed to minerals that form in a rock, which are often strangely shaped and far from perfect.

Crystallography The study of crystals and the structure of minerals.

Cubic A habit in which crystals are shaped into a cube.

Density How heavy an object feels. A small, heavy rock is denser than a small, light rock. The density of an object is its weight divided by its volume (the amount of space it takes up).

Electrons   The negative particles that surround the nucleus of an atom.

Element   One "flavor" or type of atom. Atoms make up the entire universe, but there are more than 100 different kinds, each called an element. Hydrogen and carbon are two common elements.

Erosion   The slow chipping away of a rock. Wind, rain, snow, ice and all slowly chisel down the rocks on Earth's surface, chipping off tiny bits until the entire rock is gone.

Explosive volcanism   When water mixes with magma, the water turns to vapor and bubbles furiously inside the magma. When that magma erupts from a volcano, the water vapor explodes out of the lava so forcefully that it can destroy whole mountains. The eruptions of Mount St. Helens are a good example of explosive volcanism. It usually happens along subduction zones where water is sucked down into the mantle and mixed with magma.

Fan   A habit in which crystals are arranged in a fan shape.

Fault   A break in a rock. Rocks are getting squashed and ripped apart all the time as Earth's continents move around. When they are pushed or pulled too hard, they break and move along a fault, sometimes causing an earthquake. Every part of Earth's crust is split by faults, but most of these do not produce earthquakes.

Felsic   A light-colored rock that contains the minerals feldspar and quartz. Granite is a felsic rock.

Fibrous   A habit in which long, thin, hairlike crystals are meshed together.

Fluorescence   A special power of some minerals. Fluorescent minerals glow when placed beneath a special ultraviolet lightbulb.

Foliations   Patterns and lines of minerals found in some metamorphic rocks.

Fossiliferous   A term meaning "full of fossils" (especially tiny shells from sea creatures); describes some sedimentary rocks.

Fracture   A break in a rock or mineral. You can sometime tell what kind of mineral you have by how it breaks.

Gabbro   An intrusive igneous rock made of the minerals plagioclase, pyroxene, and olivine. Gabbro is like basalt that never erupted on Earth's surface. It usually has large crystals that cooled slowly underground.

Gems   Minerals that have been cut and polished so they sparkle and shine. Some minerals, like diamonds and rubies, make beautiful gems that people wear as jewelry. Other minerals, like hornblende, do not make beautiful gems because they do not sparkle when cut.

Grain   One mineral in an igneous rock. Some rocks are "coarse-grained," meaning that the minerals that make it up are large. A "fine-grained" rock is made of small minerals. In a sedimentary rock, one grain is one chipped off another rock.

Granite   An intrusive igneous rock made of the minerals quartz and feldspar, with small bits of biotite or hornblende, too. Granite is one of the most common rocks on Earth, making up most of Earth's continental crust.

Groundwater   Water that trickles through tiny cracks in rocks. Groundwater—especially warm groundwater—can chip atoms and molecules off rocks, carry them along, and drop them elsewhere, making new minerals.

Habit   The shape of a mineral. Because each mineral has one molecular structure, that mineral usually has the same shape, making habit a good way to identify a mineral.

Hardness   A measure of how difficult it is to scratch a mineral. Diamond is a hard mineral; talc is a soft mineral.

Hydrothermal   A term meaning "from hot water." Hydrothermal minerals form when hot groundwater flows through tiny cracks in the rocks, chipping off different molecules and dropping them elsewhere. Some of Earth's most important minerals are often found in hydrothermal deposits, including gold and copper minerals.

Igneous   Minerals or rocks that form from lava (above ground) or magma (below ground).

Inner Core   The innermost part of the Earth: a hot, solid ball of iron and nickel.

Intermediate   Igneous rocks that are somewhere between light-colored felsic and dark-colored mafic, and can contain both mafic minerals like pyroxene and olivine and felsic minerals like quartz and feldspar. Andesite is an intermediate rock.

Intrusive igneous rocks   Rocks that form from magma, cooling slowly underground. They are called "intrusive" because the magma bubbles up into rocks that are already there, *intruding* on them. They are called "igneous" for the Latin word meaning "from fire."

Lava   Liquid rock that bubbles up out of the ground. While underground, the liquid rock is called magma. As soon as it erupts onto the surface, it is called lava. Lavas cool into igneous rocks like basalt or rhyolite.

Layered   Striped rocks. Sedimentary rocks are often layered because sand or mud will be laid down on a lake bottom, and then covered with multiple new layers of sand or mud. The resulting rock looks striped.

Luster   A mineral's "shininess." Some minerals are as shiny as mirrors; others are not shiny at all. Luster is therefore a good way to tell minerals apart.

Mafic   A mineral or rock that is rich in the elements magnesium and iron. Olivine and pyroxene are considered mafic minerals, and basalt, which is rich in olivine and pyroxene, is considered a mafic rock. Mafic rocks are usually dark colored.

Magma   Liquid rock that is still underground. When magma cools underground, it forms intrusive igneous rocks like gabbro and granite. When it erupts onto the Earth's surface, we call it lava, and it cools to form volcanic igneous rocks like basalt and rhyolite.

Magnetic   A special property of some metallic minerals. Magnetic minerals will attract a magnet if one is placed next to it.

Mantle   The middle part of the Earth, below Earth's crust but above the core. The mantle is made of a neon green rock called peridotite and is so warm that it can ooze like butter.

Mass   The weight of an object.

Metallic   Like metal. Metallic minerals are made of metallic elements like iron, nickel, or aluminum. They usually behave like metals, too: They look shiny like metal, are hard like metal, and are sometimes magnetic like some metals.

Metamorphic   Rocks or minerals that form from metamorphism.

Metamorphism   The slow rearranging of atoms and molecules due to heating or squishing minerals. Metamorphism changes old minerals into new minerals and old rocks into different kinds of rocks.

Minerals   The building blocks of rocks. A mineral is a solid object that is made of *one kind of molecule*, stacked over and over again in a certain way. An object cannot be a mineral unless it is nonliving and made by nature. Quartz is a good example of a mineral: It is made of one molecule (SiO_2) that is stacked in a structured way.

Mohs' hardness scale   A system that geologists use to describe the hardness of a mineral; see *hardness*

Molecule   A few atoms held together by bonds. The most famous molecule is water (H_2O): two hydrogen atoms bonded to an oxygen atom. Molecules stack to make minerals.

Mud   Tiny sediments chipped off rocks and mixed with water. When pressed hard enough, mud turns into the rock mudstone.

Oceanic crust   The rocks that make up the ocean floors. Oceanic crust is usually basalt, with a few other rocks here and there. Unlike the thick (20-mile, or 35 km) continental crust, oceanic crust is usually only about 4 miles (6.4 km) thick.

Outer core   The outer part of Earth's core, the center of the Earth. The outer core is made of boiling-hot liquid iron.

Peridotite   The rock that makes up Earth's mantle. Peridotite is a neon green rock made almost entirely of the mineral olivine.

Phyllosilicate minerals   Minerals formed from silica tetrahedra that are stacked like long sheets of paper.

Piezoelectric effect   The ability of some minerals to produce an electric field when compressed.

Plate   A segment of Earth's crust. Plates are usually made of ocean crust and continental crust. A plate starts at a spreading center, where ocean crust is born out of the mantle, and ends at a subduction zone or continental collision zone.

Plate tectonics   The movement of plates across Earth's surface. Spreading centers are constantly pushing plates away, and subduction zones are constantly sucking plates down. The result is that plates move across Earth's surface all the time, pulling their continents along with them.

Platy   A habit in which a rock or mineral is shaped like a stack of thin plates or sheets of paper.

Porphyritic texture   A dotted pattern that develops in some igneous rocks. Sometimes, while a magma is sitting underground, waiting to erupt, some of its minerals cool and form large blobs. When the magma erupts, the rest of the minerals cool so quickly that they cannot form large grains, and the resulting rock has some large grains surrounded by little ones, making it look polka-dotted. This happens frequently with basalt and rhyolite, two common volcanic igneous rocks.

Precipitation   The formation of minerals from a liquid. Often, if two molecules are floating around in water and meet up, they will connect to form a mineral. The new mineral is too heavy to float in the water and sinks to the bottom: This process is precipitation.

Pressure   How squished an object is. If you placed a small rock on a loaf of bread, the loaf would feel very little pressure. If you placed a heavy rock on a loaf of bread, it would be completely squished because of the increased pressure. The same is true for rocks. Rocks deep underground have more stuff piled on top of them and so feel more pressure—they are more squished.

Radial   A habit in which crystals fan out in a circle, starting from a central point.

Radioactive   A special property of some elements and minerals. Some elements, like uranium, give off tiny bits of invisible light, called radiation. A little radiation cannot hurt you, but lots of radiation can cause cancer or other diseases. Radioactive minerals must be handled carefully, but they are rare, and you probably will not find any in your backyard.

Rock   A hard substance made up of one kind of mineral, or many different kinds of minerals.

Rock cycle   The continuous birth and destruction of rocks.

Schistosity   A texture that some rocks have. Minerals in a rock that are lined up and look like book pages have a strong schistosity. The metamorphic rock schist is the classic example.

Sedimentary   A rock or mineral that forms from sediments or molecules that are chipped off some other rock and set down elsewhere. Usually, water is doing the chipping, but some sedimentary rocks form when wind drops lots of sand in one place.

Sediments   A sediment is a bit of sand that wind, rain, or ice chipped off a rock. Sediments can be tiny—like silt or mud—

or huge, like pebbles. Sediments pile up in some areas, form-ing sand dunes or muddy puddles. If squished hard enough, the sediments can harden into sedimentary rocks like sand-stone or mudstone.

Seismic waves   Waves of energy that travel through the Earth's interior.

Silica tetrahedron   A molecule made of four oxygen atoms that form a pyramid, with a silicon atom trapped inside. The silica tetrahedron is one of the most important molecules in geology because it is the basis for so many of Earth's minerals.

Spreading center   A split in one of Earth's oceans where new rocks are born. Spreading centers form where convection cells meet the surface, ripping Earth's crust apart. Magma from the mantle bubbles up at the spreading center to form new ocean crust.

Streak test   A mineralogical test. Many minerals change color when you grind them up into tiny bits. By scraping a min-eral along a streak plate (a small tile), you leave small bits behind that show the change in color. This is a handy test to use in identifying minerals.

Striations   Small grooves on the surface of a mineral.

Subduction   The slow process of shoving a slab of ocean crust underneath another slab of crust. When an ocean plate runs into another ocean plate or into a piece of continent, it is pushed down into the mantle. As it goes down, it heats up and melts, producing magma that rises toward the surface again. The magma can erupt on the surface from a volcano or cool slowly underground to form a rock like granite.

Tabular   A habit in which a rock or mineral is shaped like a compressed shoebox.

Texture   The patterns that minerals make in a rock. Sometimes minerals will line up to make a foliation texture or line up in long sheets to make a schistosity.

Ultraviolet   A kind of light. Ultraviolet light can make fluorescent minerals glow.

Vesicular texture   A bubbly pattern often seen in basalt or other volcanic rocks. A vesicular texture forms when a magma rich in water erupts onto land. The water turns to gas and blows away, leaving behind a tiny hole. Basalts and rhyolites commonly have a vesicular texture.

Viscous   Thick and slow to flow. A viscous lava is one that is thick like molasses and does not flow easily. Rhyolite tends to be very viscous, whereas basalt is less viscous.

Volcanic igneous rock   A rock that forms from lava erupted from a volcano. Basalt and rhyolite are both volcanic igneous rocks.

Volume   The amount of space an object takes up.

Weathering   See *Erosion*.

Bibliography

▲

Bott, Martin. *The Interior of the Earth*. New York: Elsevier, 1982.

Deer, W.A. et al. *The Rock-Forming Minerals*. New York: Longman Group Limited, 1992.

Hurlbut, Cornelius. *Minerals and Man*. New York: Random House, 1968.

Klein, Cornelius. *Manual of Mineral Science*. New York: John Wiley and Sons, 2002.

Mineralogy Database Online. "Diamond Mineral Data." Available Online. URL: http://webmineral.com/data/Diamond.shtml.

——. "Graphite Mineral Data." Available Online. URL: http://webmineral.com/data/Graphite.shtml.

Pough, Fredrick H. *Rocks and Minerals*. Boston: Houghton Mifflin Company, 1996.

Presnall, Dean. "Phase Diagrams of Earth-Forming Minerals." In *Mineral Physics and Crystallography*. Edited by Thomas J. Ahrens. Washington, D.C.: American Geophysical Union, 1995.

Said, Hakim Mohammad. *Al-Biruni: His Times, Life, and Works*. Karachi, Pakistan: Hamdard Academy, 1981.

Walsh, James Joseph. *Catholic Churchmen in Science*. Philadelphia, Penn.: American Ecclesiastical Review, 1906.

Young, Edward. *Innovations in Earth Sciences*. Santa Barbara, Calif.: Helicon Publishing, 1999.

Further Reading

▲

BOOKS

Blobaum, Cindy. *Geology Rocks! 50 Hands-on Activities to Explore the Earth*. New York: Williamson Publishing, 1999.

Farndon, John. *How It Works: How the Earth Works*. New York: Reader's Digest.

Hooper, Meredith. *The Pebble in My Pocket: A History of Our Earth*. New York: Viking Juvenile, 1996.

National Audubon Society. *Field Guide to North American Rocks and Minerals*. Washington, D.C.: Alfred A. Knopf, 1979.

O'Brien-Palmer, Michelle. *How the Earth Works*. Chicago: Chicago Review Press, 2002.

Schneider, Stuart. *Collecting Fluorescent Minerals*. Atglen, Penn.: Schiffer Publishing, 2004.

Silver, Donald. *The Amazing Earth Model Book*. New York: Scholastic Press, 1999.

VanCleave, Janice. *Earth Sciences for Every Kid*. New York: Jossey-Bass Publishers, 1991.

WEB SITES

Geology for Kids
http://kidsgeo.com
A fun introduction to the basic concepts of geology, with games and demonstrations.

Mineralogy Database Online
http://webmineral.com
An extensive database of minerals organized by their different properties.

Mineralogy Database
http://www.mindat.org
This website includes a database of minerals, a listing of news about minerals, and several discussion boards about mineralogy.

Mineral Matters
http://www.sdnhm.org/kids/minerals/how-to.html
Run by the San Diego Natural History Museum, this site provides an overview of mineral properties and how to identify different minerals.

The Rock Identification Key
http://rockhounds.com/rockshop/rockkey/
The Rock Key is an interactive method of identifying different rocks and minerals in a step-by-step process.

Picture Credits

▲

Index

▲

About the Author

▲

SELBY CULL studies Martian rocks and minerals at Washington University in St. Louis. She received her master's in science writing from MIT and has written for geology and astronomy magazines such as *Sky & Telescope* and *Geotimes*. Rocks and minerals—on Earth and beyond—are the great joy of her life.